# Sunlight in the Darkness

## Anne Cognito

My life as a trans woman in the shadows

All rights reserved; no part of this publication may be reproduced or transmitted by any means, electronic, mechanical, or otherwise, without the prior permission of the author.

Copyright © 2013 Anne Cognito

ISBN 978-1-291-60598-3

# Contents

Foreword......................................................................................5
Pride............................................................................................7
Sex change spy ........................................................................11
Football....................................................................................17
Surfer girl.................................................................................20
Snooker....................................................................................24
A crack in my life ...................................................................31
Norway ....................................................................................37
Coming out ..............................................................................49
Rhodes .....................................................................................52
Coolest student ever................................................................56
Support.....................................................................................59
Local glory...............................................................................64
For Face Sake .........................................................................69
I am a woman .........................................................................81
Legally me ..............................................................................86
What's your real name?...........................................................92
The fear....................................................................................96
The party................................................................................101
Merry Christmas everyone ...................................................107
The naked truth .....................................................................113
Dilated to meet you...............................................................116
Boobs.....................................................................................121
Stereotypes............................................................................129
Marathon girl ........................................................................133
Coming out, part 2 ................................................................151
Can I help you sir?................................................................157
Speech therapy......................................................................159
Coming out, part 3 ................................................................163
A letter to my nephews ........................................................169
You're not trans anymore......................................................174
The Maui turtle .....................................................................178
Conclusion: coming out, part 4............................................181

# Foreword

It's Saturday 27th July 2013 and I'm walking with a crowd of awesome people through the streets of Brighton on the south coast of England. It's a beautiful sunny day and off-the-shoulder sun dresses seem the fashion choice of the day for the girls, while the guys all seem to have the look of self-assured and effortless chic. The casual observer may note that we are a stylish bunch of people, but would they notice we are all transgender? With the exception of one or two partners and allies we were all assigned a different gender at birth to the one we identify as and now present to the outside world.

This is Transpride - the first event of its kind in the UK to promote equality and raise the profile of trans men and women. We are out and proud, which for some of us is quite a step forward. The world is a harsh place for trans people, and many of us prefer to stay hidden in plain sight, with few knowing we are trans. There is much prejudice against trans people, and those brave enough to be open about being transgender risk all manner of discrimination, at the milder end of the scale, to violence at the extreme end. It is hoped that events like Transpride can raise awareness of trans issues in wider society and improve the lives of trans people everywhere.

I am one of the hidden ones. I transitioned in the 80s in very different times. It felt like there was no choice but to hide. Trans people were the stuff of salacious stories in the tabloid press. We were the butt of jokes. We existed on the fringes of society. Any dream of holding down a regular job, simply living a normal life, meant starting afresh and keeping your former life secret. For thirty years I hid; it wore me down.

This is 2013 and change is in the air. Earlier in the year there was a 150-strong protest outside the offices of the Observer newspaper, after a journalist published a vile transphobic piece denouncing trans people. Trans and non-trans people stood side by side in protest, and the newspaper withdrew the piece, issuing an apology. Then came the staggering 200,000 signature petition calling for the dismissal of a Daily Mail journalist, after his campaign against a trans school teacher eventually led to her suicide. The public were starting to take notice of how the press treated trans people and were now prepared to do something.

Over the years I had been a casual observer, resigned to the fact that society would never accept me as an equal, were they to know I'm trans. Now though I was starting to see change; I was reaching out to other trans people via the Internet and realising that there was a battle out there, and one that was worth fighting. I'd been beaten down over the years, by the reactions of my family and former friends to me being trans, but now I was regaining pride in who I am and wanting to show that I wasn't prepared to hide anymore.

It felt like Transpride was a watershed moment for me, like I was shaking off thirty years of oppression. In reality, it was the end of a journey that had started less than two years earlier, at my father's funeral...

# Pride

I've changed.

That might seem an obvious thing to say, but in the last two years I've grown more than in the previous twenty. Two years ago I was an outwardly happy trans woman of twenty-seven butterfly years, living a cis-female[1] existence. I had lots of friends but led an often solitary life – something that had been commented on. I was hiding a secret, a dirty secret, something that had blighted my whole apparently happy life. No matter what I achieved, and there was much to be thankful for, there was always the thought that I didn't deserve it. Somehow I would always be that shameful excuse for a woman: the evil daughter, sister, aunt, whom should never be spoken of.

Then I attended my father's funeral.

My father: the man who had not spoken to or seen me in twenty-eight years. He had not uttered a word about me in that time. He'd written a will so that he could explicitly write me out of it. There was no mention of me. I no longer existed.

Actually he had contacted me via my extended family ten years ago, to tell me not to turn up to my mother's funeral. He'd forbidden me any contact with my mother. The one phone conversation I'd had with her had ended abruptly:
"Got to go. Your father's coming up the garden!"

---

[1] *cis* comes from the Latin prefix meaning 'On the same side as' and simply means non-trans. If someone is cis-gendered or cis-female then their gender identity is in line with their birth-assigned gender.

Her death was a long and painful one at the hands of pancreatic and liver cancer. In her final hours she was asked by my sister-in-law if she'd like to see me: her body language said yes, but looking at my father she said no. She died never seeing the beautiful confident woman her confused awkward child had become.

I had never met my sister-in-law. My brother was away at university when I transitioned. I had tried to contact him, but back then that meant letter writing and I didn't have his address. I had written to him via my parents and they had torn up the letters. He was deeply hurt in the ensuing maelstrom of accusations and misinformation. When the Gender Identity Clinic contacted him to suggest he should let me get on with transition away from my parents and not try to contact me, he obeyed. Despite my continued efforts across the years to get him to let me back into his life, he told his children and in-laws he was an only child. I no longer existed.

My father was a monster. Everything I did that was against the gender norm would receive swift corrective actions. By 1960s parenting standards he probably would not have been judged harshly; by any modern standards, this was child abuse. From my earliest years my behaviour was feminine, but of course this was forbidden. Putting on your mother's dress and saying "look mummy I'm pretty just like you" would be considered normal for a young girl, but for a son it was a reason for a hard smack. I should have been his little princess but instead he was my ogre. I had to modify my behaviour to what he considered acceptable, and hide the real me. The constant emotional and physical battering wore me down until I was ashamed of everything I was. I was left not with cherished childhood memories of love and support, but with painful images of cowering in hiding places, such as under the dressing table, trying to escape his rage.

My last indirect contact with my father was twenty nine years ago. After university I'd moved to London to begin the transition I'd been planning all my life, and I never went back home again. I had to be free of my father to be who I truly was. I had told my parents about my transition plans and as expected they were outraged and completely unsupportive. One day I arrived home at my flat in London to find that my father had sent his brothers-in-law down from the Midlands to drag me back 'home' so that they could control and correct me. When I talk about this incident I refer to it as 'the kidnap squad'. I was terrified. Fortunately my uncles saw sense and didn't carry through his plan. It was however the final straw that made me run away and cut contact from everyone who'd ever known me. That was the lowest point of my life; my journey back started there.

Fast forward twenty-seven years and I'm driving to the monster's funeral. I'm with my aunt: my angel - the one person who supported me through the fire storm. When she met butterfly-me for the first time after nine years of exile, she said something that makes me cry to this day:
"You're lovely. I totally understand now. This is the real you."

I'd mentally rehearsed the funeral for days. This was my chance to show I wasn't beaten; I'd won. I'm a successful professional woman. I'm not the figure of ridicule and hate that the monster now lying in his coffin would have everyone believe.

My attire was very deliberate: an expensive but conservative ruched black dress, knee length with just a hint of cleavage showing. I'd dressed it down with an elegant draped grey cardigan, appropriate for the suddenly autumnal weather. Black patent kitten heels, pearl earrings, and understated makeup completed the look.

As I got out of the car I saw my childhood neighbours for the first time in thirty years. My heart quickened. Alan looked at me enquiringly and my smile confirmed his suspicions.
"Oh mate, you look amazing" and then an embarrassed blush as he corrected himself.
"Er, love, I mean…"
His wife Julie took control:
"Darling! Your figure! Do you work out?"

So far so good then!

I'd been ordered by my brother to stay in the shadows and not cause a fuss. I'm not sure what he'd expected, but it was becoming clear that anyone who might have taken exception to my presence had no idea who I was.

I had my allies. I may have painted a picture of total rejection but hostility had only been from my parents and brother. I wasn't sure who knew about me on my father's and brother's side of the family, but everyone on my mother's side knew about me or had met me, and without exception were loving and welcoming.

We walked into the chapel, my cousin holding my hand, and sat four rows back. 'The family' – my brother, with his wife, sons and his sister-in-law, all of whom I'd never seen before, filed in. I wasn't sure which of the women was my sister-in-law but figured she must be the one next to my brother. (It later transpired I was wrong). My brother saw me, the real me for the first time ever, and recognised me. He nodded.

After a short service we made our way to the graveside. Again, I was in the shadows, with my supporters. My brother made eye contact but this time beckoned me forward. I stood almost at graveside with 'the family'.

What followed was for me a moment of high comedy. As the minister uttered the words "Ashes to ashes.." an autumnal squall picked up the fallen leaves, spiralled them at the minister and dumped them on top of the coffin. It was like a scene from a horror movie. I expected a voice to boom down: "You are judged to have led an evil life and are eternally damned!"

At the conclusion of the service my brother grabbed my hand and held it tight, whispering the first words he'd said to me face to face:
"Thank you."

A week later my angel aunt met another aunt from my father's side of the family. I'd always assumed everyone knew what had happened to me.
"I'm surprised [insert male name here] wasn't at the funeral."
"She was!"
My aunt then proceeded to give a potted history of my life to my estranged family member. Her reply I will always cherish:
"Is that all it was? I assumed it was something serious".


I've changed.

I am a proud trans woman. I hold my head high. The events of my life have shaped me and made me the person I am today. I like that person.

# Sex change spy

*November 1984*

I'm a rock star. I'm standing on a stage in an auditorium in the bowels of US Missile Command receiving a standing ovation. I'm the star of the conference. I've just delivered a technical analysis of intelligence data to top US brass, proving that a foreign power has broken an international treaty, by concealing the true capabilities of their weapon systems. I could see the jaws dropping as I placed my conclusions foil on the overhead projector. I even had to do an encore, ad-libbing with blackboard and chalk the further research I'd done since sending the foils in the diplomatic pouch three months before.

I was a bit of a spy cliché: recruited into the British intelligence services from Cambridge University. I was a gifted mathematician with a flare for problem solving. I was locked in a metal box all day, fed data by our American friends, and all that was asked was that I work out what all the numbers and squiggles meant and turn them into a technical spec for a foreign weapon system. I delivered! Boy was I good at this job!

Back at US Missile Command let's consider what's wrong with the picture: to my audience I'm a young well-groomed British guy, perhaps a little effeminate, but it's the 80s and permed hair is not uncommon. Some might notice that I don't seem capable of growing a beard or any other form of facial adornment. What I'm more concerned about is that the auditorium lights don't shine through my shirt and reveal that I've strapped my A cups down with crêpe bandage.

That evening I'm the toast of the celebration meal. I'm introduced to my CIA handler, whom I won't name, but I had a wry smile years later when I heard the name of the lead character in '24'! He discusses my very modest UK salary and offers me a job on five times the money with the CIA. Holy crap! This would be brilliant if it wasn't for the bombshell I was about to drop on everyone on my return to England. To further dent my confidence in my forthcoming out-coming, he tells a joke at the dinner table:
"How do you perform a sex change with a drinking straw?

Stick it up his nose and suck his brains out."
While you're reeling from the misogyny of that, I should perhaps make the historical observation that societally only trans women existed in the early 80s, so 'sex change'[2] implied male to female. Well done all you trans men for staying out of the tabloids!

I arrived back in the UK full of bravado, my ego the size of Macclesfield. Now was my time. They love me. I'm indispensable: the star analyst. Time to lay out my plans for personal development.

Oh my god, the shit-storm that followed! They panicked.

I broke the news of my transition to my manager, who discussed it with our RAF liaison, the Squadron Leader. It then went to the Wing Commander, and, oh crap, on to the Group Captain. I'd hate to call the RAF chicken, but there were several examples of the headless variety running around that day.

Within an hour, I'd been escorted under guard back to my desk to grab my bag and hand over the combination to my various document lockers. I was then marched out of the building and never saw my place of work again. Actually, I lie: I was to see that place one more time three years later, but let's move on.

I bloody loved my job. It was what I thought was the perfect job to transition in. I had necessarily limited contact with people outside of my office. We were not allowed to talk about our job to anyone. It was the perfect job for some peace and quiet and anonymity. Given the work I did, my main fear was not how the Ministry Of Defence would react, but what the tabloids might do if they got hold of my story. Apart from books by April Ashley and Jan Morris, the tabloids had been my main source of info growing up. They loved a juicy headline!

---

[2] You will not usually hear a trans person use the term 'sex change' - it's a throwback term used by the press, generally indicative of bad journalism.

Now I was out on my own. Technically I still had a job, being on 'gardening leave', but they made it quite clear that they weren't going to support this situation for long. Transition started now. They had just brought my plans forward by several months.

*Arse! I need to get all my documents sorted out! Help!*

The MoD very graciously found me a job at a defence firm doing 'similar' work to what I had been doing: analysing data from weapon tests, but this time *our* weapon tests, and with a manual to tell you what all the data meant. In any other situation I'd have said it was beneath me, but I was now caught up in a stealth[3] transition, and I didn't really worry too much about how challenging the work wasn't. I may have been thrown onto the streets but it's rare one can transition in stealth and I seemed to have landed on my feet. I had a moment of panic when I was asked for my degree and A-level certificates and realised they were in my old name, but fortunately I was able to keep delaying them until the new ones arrived a few weeks later. I was asked for my passport: it showed my correct name, but back then we weren't allowed to have *female* on it. It didn't say *male*, but it was different to a regular passport. Would they notice?

I lived in constant fear of being outed, but somehow I coped. I made some really good friends and transition went really well. *Wow, this stealth business is easy!* A year later I had my surgery, and arranged some extended time off. All went well with only one guy asking what the operation was for. I replied that it was a gynaecological procedure and he shut up immediately, rather red faced, and clearly wishing he hadn't asked. One of my friends seemed overly concerned about my levels of pain, which struck me as odd, but no one asked any probing questions.

On my return to work I had my one really awkward moment. I was sitting at my computer terminal with my back to everyone, when the new girl rushed in and standing back to back with me, announced to the office:

---

[3] I don't particularly like the word stealth, but it's the common word for living as your identified gender without others knowing your trans history.

"Hey everyone, I've just heard there's a transsexual[4] working on our floor. Where are they?"

I wanted the ground to open up and swallow me. I was bright red and sweating but kept looking straight ahead at the screen pretending to work. Curiously, nothing further was said, and it never occurred to me at the time why there was silence.

It would take a series of job interviews before I realised the significance of that event.

I was now settled in to life as a female and enjoying it to the full. I was taking up sports. Sport! Me! I had a body I could enjoy doing stuff in. Yay!

Time to do something about my career.

I signed up to a recruitment agency and started going to job interviews. I interviewed well: before them sat a bright bubbly girl, happy with life, and keen to do something with it. Who couldn't love her? At each interview I was offered the job on the spot, but being defence jobs they had to say "subject to paperwork". Still having a security clearance, albeit one much lower than I had at the MoD, I knew that they had to get me cleared to work at the new firm. Curiously, a few weeks after each interview I'd get an apologetic rejection letter. Three interviews in, and I was starting to get concerned.

One day an official letter from MoD head office arrived on my door step. I was invited back to my old place of work "to discuss your recent job interviews". I started shaking as the truth dawned on me: the puppet masters had been pulling my strings.

---

[4] I'm quoting her. I avoid using transsexual, due to the loaded nature of 'sexual', and I certainly never use it as a noun. I'm a trans woman; I'll just about accept *transsexual woman,* but I'm not *a transsexual*. Note also that I'm not a *transwoman*, as this seems to imply something separate from *woman*. I'm a woman first, trans second.

The head of security was situated in the first room on the first floor: room 101! Would it be rats they had for me, or would I get surrounded by creepy little guys who press their noses into your boobs on packed tube trains? (Is that just me, or does it happen to everyone?)

In a very perfunctory 'interview', I was told by a subhuman with no personality, that I had been denied a security clearance for my prospective jobs because of my failure to reveal my trans status. I was then told that in order to be considered for a clearance, I must:
- Submit to a full medical examination (translation: lift up your skirt and drop your panties, dear).
- Agree to full disclosure of my trans status to the work force.

As you can imagine, I wasn't best pleased. On questioning why I was ok for a clearance in my current job, he then revealed that they had told all my colleagues about me! My supposed stealth transition had been conducted in full disclosure. At the time I was horrified, but I've since come to realise what a brilliant bunch of people I had been working with: no one had ever said anything to suggest they knew I was trans.

My interview ended with one of the few times I ever raise my voice to anyone. I remember clearly the last two words I said to my overlord: "FUCK OFF!"

On the way back to the train station I picked up The Guardian newspaper, saw an advert for a job with a major IT firm, and within a week had been offered a job. I regretfully turned my back on all my former colleagues, and have been living a stealth life in that job ever since.

Many years later, the MoD came back to haunt me once more when my new employers requested I be cleared for work on a government project. I nervously filled in the forms, leaving certain bits blank, with caveats about personal information I'd only discuss face to face, suspecting that I'd get flagged up anyway. I was right. Two weeks into the supposed three-month process, I got a call from my old puppet masters. I had been given a clearance with no strings attached! The man at the other end of the phone was actually quite pleasant:
"I think you'll find society has moved on somewhat since the 1980s"

Society maybe has moved on, but I wonder if the MoD really has. Fortunately the government contract never materialised and I never had to work again in a secure environment. My trust in the MoD has been lost forever. I wrote to the MoD recently, trying to get clarification on just what they meant by that last statement, and asked for a full apology for how they treated me previously: I never heard back from them.

# Football

*1975*

Testosterone. I hate that stuff! It seems to turn teenage boys into animals.

"Man on! Man on!" screamed in such an aggressive tone. What the hell does it mean anyway? I have my arms shielding my head, as the ball is coming straight at me. I look away as the ball whistles past me. I've managed to avoid it hitting me once more.

"You fucking poof!".

My poor team lost the toss. The other team had first pick of players, my team had the last choice. They ended up with me.

There's a box painted on the grass around our goal. This seems to be the safest place to stand: the ball rarely gets down here. Trouble is, when it does, there's all the shouting and kicking, with the ball zooming past at head height. It's dangerous, but only for mercifully brief periods, until the ball goes out or ends up in the net.

Now the teacher is having a go at me. It seems ok for teachers here to carry on the bullying meted out by the pupils.

"Move Cognito!"[5]

I jog to the edge of the box, which has the advantage of getting me away from the ball approaching down the other side of the pitch. The danger passes, as does the teacher, and I wander back towards the goalkeeper for a

---

[5] That's not actually what he said. You did realise Anne Cognito is a pen-name?

chat. This process repeats itself a few times, and I'm getting the hang of getting out of the way of the ball and goalkeeper.

"Cognito! I've had enough of you! Start running round the edge of the pitch. Now!"

I'm not a runner; I'm a swimmer. I'm actually quite a good, well trained, swimmer. What leg muscles I have though aren't used to propelling me on land. I jog along the edge of the pitch, but stop to get my breath when the teacher isn't looking. The kids are all laughing at me. This is humiliating. When is this going to end? Please blow the whistle.

It's a damp misty day. It's muddy. It's cold. I'm cold. I'm miserable. This is hell.

Finally the whistle blows. At last.

And so to the showers.

Out of the frying pan...

I hate the showers. The ceramic corridor of humiliation and shame. I don't use them if at all possible. If I keep my underpants on they just laugh at me even more. I can't stand anyone seeing me naked. It doesn't help being the youngest in the year, having skipped a year in junior school. The others are all bigger and hairier; I'm almost hairless. I don't want to be big and hairy, but it just makes it easier for them to ridicule me. Why do they all seem so comfortable naked?

It's easier just to avoid the showers completely. I'm muddy though. I try to wipe away what mud I can with my shirt. I then towel myself down. My underpants stay on.

Fully clothed at last, I catch the bus across town, and arrive home destroyed. Before I do anything else I go to the bathroom to cut today's chewing gum out of my hair. It turns my stomach to imagine it coming from someone else's mouth. I've learnt not to try to pull it out, as it just gets more tangled and hurts too much. It's easier to just accept it and wait till I get home to cut it out neatly. I don't tell Mum. I flush it away and move on. Today is different though.

I go into my parents' bedroom. Somehow this makes more sense than going to my own room. I curl up on the bed and stare at the bedspread, trying to ignore the world, and the voices screaming at me, telling me I'm a freak. I feel the heat in my face as the blood pressure rises and I flush. I'm shaking. The tears roll down my cheeks and onto the bed. I try to keep quiet, in case Mum hears me. She's calling me for tea though. I don't reply. I can't go downstairs like this.

Mum's now standing over me, asking what's wrong, using words like "darling" and "love". I don't really feel any love though. I feel so incredibly alone in the heart of my family. I feel completely isolated. I can't tell her what's wrong. I suppose I can tell her some of what has happened, but I can't tell her what's really wrong. I can't tell her *I'm* what's wrong. I can't tell her I'm a freak. I can never tell her.

Through the sobbing, gulping and sniffing, I manage to get the word out:

"Football."

# Surfer girl

*November 1990*

It's five years after transition and my obsession with sport and fitness, and more specifically windsurfing, has led me here to a beach in the Caribbean, competing in the World Windsurfing Championships. What the hell am I doing here? Do I deserve to be here? What if I'm found out?

On the beach, the German team are reading a windsurfing magazine with an article entitled "Eine Frau wie Anna". It's an exposé on a, perhaps willing, trans female recreational windsurfer. Trans people who dare to indulge in something like windsurfing are apparently newsworthy, even if they are doing it just as a hobby. The German guys are enjoying sexualising and ungendering[6] her. I can't understand exactly what they are saying, given my schoolgirl German, but it is not complimentary. I'm trying to lurk without seeming obvious. I'm very nervous. One of them smiles at me; I manage to grimace back.

A Swedish woman has just been taken to hospital after treading on a lionfish in the shallows. If the blades of grass on the lawn don't give you paper cuts on your feet, then the ants crawling through them will get you with their stings. I've just had a close encounter with a barracuda. Now I have the psychological onslaught of six transphobic Germans to deal with. This is a hostile place.

I hope no one demands a sex test. Do we even have them in this branch of the sport? Windsurfing is an Olympic sport, but my discipline is a more exciting and modern version, more familiar to the average guy at the beach. (I deliberately said 'guy' there, more on that later). Trans people are effectively banned from the Olympics, given the need to 'pass' a sex test. I guess I would be allowed to compete as male, but that isn't just a social

---

[6] The process of looking for the little tells that reassure the transphobic onlooker that the person is not the gender he or she says they are.

inconvenience but a physical impossibility: I don't have a man's strength. It is effectively a ban. It wouldn't be until Sydney 2000 that trans people could compete, provided they are two years post-surgery. (This remains a contentious issue for trans men due to the risk and cost of phalloplasty).

Back at the beach it's my first taste of competition at this level. That in itself would be enough to make someone nervous. Windsurfing is a technical sport and you have to be relaxed or you will make big mistakes; one fall and your race is over. With all the baggage that I was carrying, feeling the eyes of the male competitors were all focused on me, ungendering me with every glance, how could I hope to finish anywhere but the back of the field? It would take another year before I felt the entitlement to compete equally, and another year to have the confidence to fight the rampant sexism in the sport.

Let's deal with the sexism first.

It took me a while to realise that what I perceived as transphobia was actually plain sexism. When you're standing on a beach in a gale, wearing an unflattering wetsuit, your nose red with cold and your hair plastered across your face, you are in stark contrast to the images of 'windsurfing' women plastered across the pages of the windsurfing press. The only female professional windsurfers that even got a mention in magazines were the pretty ones with ample figures. Women outnumbered men in the adverts, but who were these women with amazing skills of being able to lie on a board or hold a mast seductively? I don't recall seeing any of them on the professional circuit.

No one was ever going to see me as pretty while I was competing on the water, but I didn't fair much better off it. I would finish a competition weekend with salt crusted hair - often nowhere to shower - and would be walking through the predominantly male crowd to collect my trophy looking far from my best. On one such occasion, as I walked up to receive my trophy, one of the guys, a British former world champion, said "It's a good job we don't give out trophies for beauty". It made me shrivel inside. He said it just loud enough for me to hear it, and for his mates to be amused by it. My lack of looks is irrelevant to my ability to windsurf. I took it as transphobic, but later I realised it was just plain misogyny.

Windsurfing is a macho extreme sport. Technique is key, but when it comes to extreme conditions, strength is a big advantage. I was a match for any man on my local beach, but at national level the gap between the men and women was clear to see, and we struggled to be taken seriously. The men outnumbered the women ten to one, which didn't help. So long as we knew our place and kept out of their way, we were tolerated. If we ever dared suggest parity in terms of prizes or having our own start line, then it was clear a different sort of line had been crossed.

All of us women became close friends and I never had any hint of a problem from the others. Once I'd realised that I was fighting the women's cause, not some imagined transphobic aggression, my confidence grew. I wore my curly permed hair like a pineapple on top of my head. I stood out.

Though the organisers could enforce the wearing of buoyancy aids, the men never wore them as it was a sign of weakness. At first, the women followed suit, but I soon realised that a buoyancy aid helped make up for lack of strength manipulating the sail in the water. I started wearing one regularly and the other women followed. I was proud of that.

I fought to make our voice heard. I was elected onto the national committee, and represented the UK at the international class association conference. Still though I struggled to gain respect as a woman in a man's world.

The nagging doubt remained: did I deserve to compete equally with other women?

Yes I did.

I hadn't carried any male privilege through to windsurfing. Due to my dysphoria I'd done very little sport at school. I hated football and would get bullied for it. My only sport was swimming, having been taught from an early age, and I competed well. However I gave that up in my teens, as I became increasingly uncomfortable with people seeing me semi-naked.

After transition I loved the skin I was in. I ran, swam, cycled, worked out and skied. I discovered I had a natural gift for windsurfing after a colleague introduced me to it. I took up competition and rose through the ranks, experiencing fully the sexism stifling many a female career. I got where I was on my own merits as a woman.

I struggled with the idea that my height was an advantage. Unlike the Olympic discipline which favoured light weight, in my arm of the sport, height gave you greater leverage to control a larger sail. I'm 5'10". The German women's world champion, who later became a good friend, was about my height. Her team mate who eventually rose to the top rank was three inches taller than me. The woman who eventually dominated the sport however, was short and stocky. It's too easy to draw conclusions about physical stature. In the world of athletics they said tall men couldn't be sprinters, but then came Usain Bolt.

Did I have a strength advantage? I only got an answer to that years later after switching to running. As my running improved I rose through the ranks just as I had done in windsurfing and was winning age group medals at county level. I was coached by a former international, along with a group of other women my age. My coach insisted I was capable of breaking 3 hours for the marathon, but I fell consistently short of that. My training partners all seemed to flourish on similar training plans. While natural talent plays a big part, I was convinced that my female musculature on a more typically male frame gave me a power to weight disadvantage.

I never won the UK windsurfing championships but was runner up on several occasions. I had some very close battles with my rivals. If I had an advantage it was hard to discern. I trained exceptionally hard, spending an hour in the gym before work each day and spending all my time on the water outside work. That got me to 14th in the world on two occasions. Always the bridesmaid, never the bride. Trans advantage? No.

I look back on my windsurfing career and wonder if I could have done more. I loved my time in the spotlight. I travelled the world. My confidence, both as a woman in a man's world and as a trans woman in society, grew and grew. I appeared on Sky TV. I represented my country both on and off the water. I helped shape the sport.

I am a proud trans woman, but more than that, I am a proud woman.

# Snooker

*April 1985*

How can a snooker match have burned into my memory so vividly? To be fair it wasn't just any snooker match but probably the greatest game of snooker ever played. It's 1985 and I'm in a holiday cottage in the Lake District with two close friends watching the World Snooker Championship final between Steve Davis and Dennis Taylor.

Throughout this book you will find me recalling the fine details of the emotionally charged moments of my life, such as what I was wearing. It's as though the electricity of a moment of high emotion has burnt the memory onto the canvas of my brain and hung there to be viewed for eternity. That snooker match was just such an occasion. However, the emotion that intensified the memory was generated not so much from the game, exciting though it was, but from what it represented in the rapidly developing drama of my life.

I was in the Lake District for my last holiday before transition. I was in boy mode as a concession to my friend Jessica who I hadn't realised thought of herself as my girlfriend. I was so naïve: I thought of her as a good friend, but she was besotted with me. She took my trans disclosure very hard: there were tears, so many tears, and not much spoken of my forthcoming transition after that. We'd planned a break in the Lake District with her mum Andrea, a good friend of mine, which isn't as odd as it seems, given how close we all were. Her mum was fine with me in girl mode, and had been out in London with me, but Jessica just couldn't cope with seeing the female me. Hence I reluctantly agreed to boy mode, as a last concession to our friendship.

Looking back I wonder if I should have been more selfish. I never pushed myself on anyone who couldn't cope with seeing the female me. My parents told me never to come back, and I didn't. I wonder how things might have turned out if I'd appeared at their door as butterfly me, but I feared the reaction that I'd had in my early childhood. Those friends who reacted badly when I came out to them, usually my female friends who had a romantic attachment to me, never saw me in female mode. I was too compliant, and too ready to walk away and not fight for recognition of my true self.

Why are people so freaked out by a change of gender presentation? The press like to talk of a *sex change* as if there's a sudden dramatic transformation, but really very little changes: the core person doesn't change and neither does their gender. Why do people freak out at a few items of female clothing and a bit of makeup? All we are trying to do is put up some cues and clues to our true gender. I didn't want drama, and apparently the weapons of peace are jeans and a chunky sweater.

So there we were for my last blast of trying to be male against all my instincts, in the Lake District in a traditional cottage just out of range of Sellafield, pretending that we were the most normal family on earth: a mother, her daughter, and her daughter's beau. I was the man of the house, swimming in a dysphoric soup. I don't think they realised the sacrifice I was making. I'd been sacked from the MoD some weeks earlier and had been living much of my life in a female role, sorting out my life, working out how best to present myself to the world, and getting ready for my first day in a new job at the defence firm the MoD had lined up for me. With each day my comfort grew as the sense of harmony, between my core female gender identity and how society treated me, grew and I developed a contentment of finally being my authentic self.

The holiday had been booked months before, and my plans back then had a transition date many months in the future. I had hoped I could have taken the holiday in girl mode, but as I would still have been working at the MoD each day in boy mode, it didn't seem such a great imposition when Jessica insisted it was strictly a boy mode deal. My coming out at the MoD and instant dismissal had changed all that though: they insisted that they couldn't keep me on 'gardening leave' for long and unless I was prepared to take the job they were offering me elsewhere then I would be making myself redundant. My choices were transition immediately and start the new job in my new gender role, start the new job in boy mode and transition according to my originally planned timescales, or refuse the job offer and get properly sacked, correction, *made redundant*. There seemed no choice but to transition immediately. My path through life as a female had begun, but unfortunately there was a large brick in the road, in the shape of our Lake District getaway.

Jessica would not budge: it was boy mode or we cancelled and lost our money.

I'm a strong woman, I always have been: my transition and abandonment by those I loved just made me stronger. Back then though I thought strength was a masculine trait, and I wanted to be cared for and protected. I felt fragile: a butterfly even in my caterpillar years. To me, we were three women on holiday together, but to them I was the man, the protector. It was a strange dynamic, having to revert to a role I had been trying to retreat from for years. This was highlighted dramatically in an incident at the top of a local mountain.

It was the end of April, with Spring in full effect. We'd had some lovely weather with bright sunshine, but one morning, as was typical of the season, it was cold and drizzly. It was decided that the order of the day would be a drive to Windermere via the scenic route over the Hardknott Pass. We didn't know at the time but the Hardknott Pass has the distinction of being the steepest road in England, not that this should task our Ford Fiesta hire car. As the only driver, it was down to me to pilot the vehicle.

The greenery of the valley seemed to sparkle in the steady drizzle as we made our way up towards the pass. We stopped briefly to gaze over the Hardknott Roman Fort half way up to the pass, but didn't stop long as we weren't really dressed for adverse weather. The road got steep and the little red Fiesta did struggle but it coped well once in its bottom gear.

"Ooh look it's snowing!" said Jessica as we got to the top of the pass. She clearly thought this was a good thing, and certainly we rarely ever saw snow in London. I guess snow at altitude in the Lake District was not unusual for April. The snow was light but persistent, and it seemed a nice contrast to the weather we'd had during the rest of the holiday. My views changed dramatically though as we turned the corner and headed down the steep road on the other side of the pass.

The snow was beginning to settle on the road, and while this wouldn't have been an issue on the flat, on a 1 in 3 gradient its effect was alarming. At the edge of the road was a very steep drop and no barrier to stop us plunging to our doom. I was trying to keep us on the safe side of the road in a car that was determined to point itself downhill regardless of which direction the front wheels happened to be pointing.

With the realisation of the extremely dangerous situation we were in, I tried to be the stoic hero that was expected of my male role. I was scared but I tried not to show this to the others. As I saw it, we had no choice but continue: if we stopped we might freeze to death as the weather closed in - we had no warm clothes with us, and no idea what the weather forecast was.

The mood in the car had now changed: no one said a word. Regardless of how calm I was managing to keep myself, the erratic motion of the car had alerted the others to the fact that I was no longer in control of the vehicle. I understood now the true meaning of 'white knuckle ride' as the others held on to the bodywork in a rigid and tense state.

I never dreamed I'd be taking a Ford Fiesta skiing. The front wheels were alternating left and right as if to echo the skis of a slalom skier battling the slopes. The road was now completely covered in snow, but mercifully I could still make out the edges of the road and was able to slalom my way cleanly down the centre.

After what seemed like an eternity, but in reality may have only been a mile, the snow started to turn back to rain, and I started to get more of a response from the steering wheel. After another mile the road had turned from white to black. After another mile my pulse was returning to normal. Jessica grabbed my arm and she gave me a relieved look of gratitude. We continued on to our destination in silence.

My gender has no bearing on my ability to drive or handle a dangerous situation. I was the driver, and it was my job to get the car down the mountainside. If there had been a man in the car though I would gladly have handed control over to him. I felt I was performing a gender role and I was very uncomfortable with that. Was I right to think like that? I certainly don't see the world like that nowadays: if I think I'm more capable than a man, which is often the case, then I will take control. Back then though I shied away from anything I saw as a male stereotype: I was being forced into a gender-role box that I was desperate to escape from. I would recoil from anything I saw as a male trait and it would send me into a spin.

Gender dysphoria, the current term used by the medical profession for what used to be known as Gender Identity Disorder, the mismatch of body and gender, to me always conjures up images of whirlpools - a spinning mire of dysphoria, trying to escape the gender-role-box society has placed me in.

How does one define gender? I have a female gender identity. I know this to be true. Some see gender as purely a performance we are forced into: girls get to play with dolls and get dressed in pink, while boys play with cars and get a muted colour palette. Some theorists tell us that we can break down gender divisions, that there are only sex differences, male and female, that gender is a construct of society and we must fight for a genderless society. I know this to be untrue. We are forced into gender-role boxes from birth, and from as far back as I can remember, I knew I didn't fit. Gender is a property of our core identity: my body may have had the outer appearance of being male, but my brain was female.

We have our gender roles to play, dolls or cars, but I saw gender as something more subtle: I knew that girls and boys were different, and I knew that I didn't belong in the male camp. At break time the playground would divide into male and female and I was in the wrong half: I wanted to play with the girls, not the boys. Whatever innate property those children over there possessed, I had it too, and they were my team, not the group of boys I was assigned to by default. I couldn't explain why I felt netball was a better sport than football, but I wanted to play netball with the girls, not football with the boys.

We do need to move forward from the idea of rigid gender roles. It is frankly ridiculous that Bic market a range of pens 'for her' in nice pretty colours. It is demeaning and contributes to the divisions in society keeping women in our place and maintaining men's dominant position. We need to stop the *pink it and shrink it* philosophy of marketing to women, which just enforces the frivolous nature of femininity. Men and women are different though, regardless of how we are brought up. We naturally assume gender roles, even when stereotypes aren't forced on us. Put small children in a room with a selection of play options, be they tea sets, cars, dolls or guns, and girls will gravitate to the girlier options and boys will go for the more boisterous options. There's no reason a boy shouldn't play with a tea set, or a girl a car, but there is a good deal of nature to enforce what is often imposed on us by nurture.

I had been nurtured as male. Whereas most boys accept their role comfortably, I had been forced into mine often at the rather too firm hand of my father. I had to struggle to break free. At the slightest display of feminine behaviour, however natural that seemed to me, my father would take swift corrective action. With each slap of the hand or beating with a slipper I would feel more and more uncomfortable. I was a square peg being beaten into a round hole and I was hurting more and more, until I could take no more and was able to escape my father's influence and run away from home to be myself.

The relief of finally being able to express my femininity albeit in initially limited circles was incredible. At last I could be myself without being judged. Even small things like getting my ears pierced or growing my hair felt like a release. I was finally breaking free of my shackles and letting the world see who I really was. As I became more adventurous in venturing out as female me, even the cries of "fucking tranny" from across the street didn't phase me. The Charing Cross Hospital Gender Identity Clinic gave me the Gender Identity Disorder diagnosis I needed and with it I was prescribed blocker pills to stop the effect of testosterone on my body, and œstrogen to give me the female figure I so dearly wanted. As the tablets took their effect my happiness grew, and I was able to pass easily as female on a daily basis. I'd got to the point where I was presenting as female in all areas of my life except work.

I had been on hormones for almost a year and had never looked back. Then came the holiday and it was back to earth with a thump. I had not realised how hard it would be to be a man for a week.

And so we return to the last day of the holiday, watching snooker in our pretty little Lake District cottage.

It's odd looking back that we should have paid any attention to a sport such as snooker, but things were different back then. These were the days before digital TV: there were only four channels and shows had huge audiences. Snooker was a major draw. The players were celebrities to the extent that they were parodied on the *Spitting Image* television show. Steve Davis was Steve 'Interesting' Davis in the famous sketch where he complains he doesn't have a nickname like Jimmy 'Whirlwind' White. Dennis Taylor was the man famous for the upside-down glasses: as a spectacle wearer he had a problem of looking over the top of his lenses and not seeing the ball, so an optician friend had turned a large framed pair of specs upside down so that the lenses protruded upwards, solving the problem.

We were working our way through the board games as we passed the night away, the television in the corner drawing us in slowly as the tension in the game increased. It was a genuinely exciting match, one which initially had seemed like a foregone conclusion: Steve Davis had pulled a long way ahead on the first day of the final, but on the second day Dennis Taylor slowly drew back until the two players were tied with one frame left to play. At this point there were eighteen million people watching the match. It had gone midnight and whoever won the next frame would be world champion.

The tension just kept increasing though, as the players started to show uncharacteristic nerves and made errors to let the other player back in. Eventually it was all down to the last ball: whoever potted the black would be world champion. Still the errors flowed as shot after shot followed, each player trying to pot the black ball. Eventually, underdog Dennis Taylor was triumphant, and we were cheering and dancing around, the sense of relief palpable.

I was relieved for a very different reason.

It was now Monday, the holiday was over, and after a few hours sleep we drove back to London. We arrived home, I dropped Andrea and Jessica off and went to return the hire car. I packed all my male clothes in a bin bag and took them down to the charity shop. From that point forward I would never present in male guise again. Sadly, because of her lack of acceptance and my reluctance to press the issue, I never saw Jessica again. Despite the huge sense of loss, it still felt worth it: my new life started there.

Monday 29th April 1985: the date of my transition.

# A crack in my life

*October 1981*

It's my second year at Cambridge University and I'm lying on my bed staring at the ceiling. My thoughts are a mess. My mind is a maelstrom of all the emotions that have been building inside me for the nineteen years of my life. I'm trans: I'm sure of this. How do I tell my parents? What am I going to do about it? Should I tell my friends? Can I transition? How do I get help? This will kill my parents. Could I continue without transitioning? Have I got the courage to kill myself? No, suicide is not an answer. Who can I talk to? Is there a helpline I can phone? I want to be a girl. I need to be a girl.

I know every detail of the crack in the ceiling: its abrupt but small changes in direction, the variations in width, the gaps where plaster has fallen away. The crack seems to grow bigger as I stare at it, and it draws me in as my thoughts take over. I've never meditated, but maybe this is how one does it: my ceiling crack is my icon, my centre of focus, my prayer beads.

My view of the crack is now starting to fade as the light is draining from the room. I'm now lying in darkness and for the first time I'm aware of the passage of time. I am suddenly shocked into action. I am now aware that I am hungry and thirsty. I am not in a healthy state of mind. I have only now realised that I have been lying on my bed, awake, staring at the ceiling, since breakfast this morning, and it is now dark. *Oh crap! I'm in a bad way. Is this what depression feels like?* It doesn't feel like depression; my mind is in turmoil, juggling all my thoughts and trying to make sense of my world. I'm now more sure than ever that I know who I am. I must seek help.

University had been my salvation and that was the watershed moment. For the first time in my life I seemed to be the mistress of my own destiny.

*I'm trans and I need to do something about it.*

It took me a year of turmoil though to reach my ceiling crack moment. I was a scholar: I'd aced the entrance exams and been awarded a bursary. It wasn't a large sum of money but it certainly helped pay the bills. In order to continue receiving the scholarship money I had to do well in the end-of-year exams. I scraped through with a third. My mum was furious: rather than try to find out the reasons behind my difficulties, she exploded with rage and ranted about how I was letting the family down. Given that I was the first member of the family to go to university, and not just any university but the finest in the world, you might have thought she'd be a little more sympathetic. That was my family: concerned totally with "what other people might think" and failing totally on all levels of love and support. What hope did I have of ever coming out to her if all she seemed concerned about was the views of others?

My relationship with my mum had been on a decline ever since I'd started university. She'd lost the person she confided in, although to me that was something of a relief as her conversations all seemed to have degenerated into endless complaints about my father and how I was the only reason they were still together; I found it all exhausting and couldn't wait to get away to university. Those conversations continued on my weekly phone calls home, but now a lot of the anger was directed at me: I'd describe the parties, the friends I'd made, the band I'd started, and she'd complain to me that I wasn't studying. Why would I talk about academic work to my mum? I wanted to talk about the exciting stuff, but it just degenerated into an argument every time. My end-of-year grade thus gave her the justification for all the shouting directed at me.

*Oh please get me away from all this so that I can sort my life out.*

My life got a whole lot better following the cathartic moment with my ceiling crack: I was able to concentrate better on my studies, our band started to take off, and I started to explore my female identity a little more, with some trips to a support group in London.

I'd always had an interest in music. I saw parallels between my musical and female aspects: both had been suppressed by my parents. I never understood why my parents would want to stifle my musical aspirations, unless they somehow saw that as one of my female attributes that had to be discouraged. When I started secondary school, the music department encouraged us take up an instrument. I came home from school announcing that I wanted to take up the violin; this would have been at no cost to my parents as it would be on a loan instrument, taught as part of school curriculum. I was told that we were not a musical family and that was the end of it. I found this baffling. Usually such decisions were based on financial considerations, but maybe they already realised they'd lose a money-based argument. When my brother came home two years later to announce in a similar fashion that he wanted to take up the bassoon, they spent over a thousand pounds buying him an instrument; baffling. In hindsight, it seems part of their efforts to control me; they claimed they had no idea I was trans but maybe their actions suggest otherwise?

I became a rebel. I was determined to learn an instrument, so my attention turned to acquiring a guitar. My father was a chain smoker, and had collected a lot of Embassy cigarette tokens. Such was the marketing of tobacco back then that to keep you locked into a brand they would give away tokens in each packet, redeemable against goods in a catalogue. The Embassy catalogue had a guitar in it, and my father had almost enough tokens to order it, but even at his rate of smoking, it would take a few more months to get enough tokens together. One day coming back from school, I noticed a wad of tokens in a junk shop window, on sale for one pound: problem solved! I bought the tokens, stole my dad's stash, and the guitar was mine.

The guitar was awful, but it was playable. Bryan Adams sings "played it 'til my fingers bled" in *Summer of '69*, and that was me, albeit in the summer of '73. The action on the guitar was really bad which meant the strings were high above the frets and took a lot of pressure to play. I was determined to learn though and a few blisters and a little blood seemed a reasonable trade. Soon I'd worked through my Bert Weedon book and was ticking off the songs in my *Beatles Complete* anthology.

I arrived at university armed with an electric guitar, having upgraded with the money I'd earned from temp jobs in what would now be called a gap year. Back then, the gap year was seen as an opportunity to get some money together to ease the burden of being a student. I was on full grant, my parents having been means-tested off the bottom of the chart, but I was thankful I'd managed to get some money together: how else would I have afforded such essentials as electric guitar and amp?

Top priority on arrival was getting a band together. I answered adverts, placed adverts and a few weeks later we had a rather unique bunch of individuals. Mike the drummer was openly gay: being out and proud in 1980 was quite a bold act, and I admired him for it. It's a shame that his friend who introduced him to us had said "Mike's gay, are you all ok with that?". Mike being out provided useful insight into the other band members. Our first lead singer Kevin came out to Mike, I later learnt. Our second lead singer Gareth was quite open about his sexuality: he was interested in experimentation - one of our songs was about a night he'd spent in bed with a man and a woman - very good lyrics! Matt, our bass player, also came out to Mike, although I only found out after we split up. Will the keyboard player seemed straight, but we later learnt that he'd been spotted in a gay club in a nearby town: that doesn't necessarily mean he was gay, but it's a fairly big clue. That just left me to come out to Mike as trans in my second year, and you have what was possibly Cambridge's only fully LGBT band.

Coming out to Mike was a very good thing for me. Mike was the first person I ever came out to, and I was so nervous. His reaction though, was unlike that of everyone else I've ever come out to: he wasn't at all freaked out by me stating I was trans, but instead tried to convince me I was gay. Mike took me to a local gay club; it was quite the experience! I was a twenty-year-old fresh-faced boy; I was very popular! Mike was very protective of me though and realised I was nervous. I just didn't seem to fit in: I wasn't particularly attracted to girls, but didn't feel attracted to guys either, at least not to a gay guy interested in me as a gay guy. I had a crush on Andy in the year below me, but he was straight. I remember turning up at his door one night to suggest we went for drinks. There was something in how I said it that made Andy say straight back "Are you asking me on a date?". I was so embarrassed. I remember though wearing Andy's leather jacket to a gig; I felt great in the jacket. I guess that's the closest I ever got to him.

I didn't have much style back then, part of my general awkwardness in all things male. Matt the bass player tried to style me, and I let him. I got rid of my glasses and wore contact lenses, something I realised would be useful in future when going out in female guise. I grew my hair a bit longer and had it styled in a soulboy cut. I started wearing more brightly coloured clothing, not exactly androgynous, but a little less drab male than I was previously accustomed to. I became rather attached to my bright-red drain-pipe jeans. At a gig in a local pub, Matt persuaded me to wear a chef's jacket with my red jeans, and I wore eyeliner for the first time. I walked across the bar to get to the stage, and a big ape of a guy blocked my path and shouted

"Are you a fuckin' poof or some'in'?"
I managed to get past him and onto the stage. Maybe once he saw I was in the band he was more accepting. That incident stayed with me though. How could I ever go out in public in makeup and a dress, if that's the reaction I got from wearing a slightly wacky outfit and eyeliner?

The band gained a bit of a following around Cambridge; we even ventured further afield and played at the University of East Anglia, supporting *Way of the West*, quite a mainstream band at the time. During that gig we got a flavour of how support acts are treated: they wouldn't let us use the monitors, and so the only sound we could hear was that reflected off the opposite wall of the hall. There was a delay in us hearing ourselves and so we couldn't play in time. After the gig, I met a school friend who was at UEA, and thinking he'd be really impressed I was in a band, I asked:
"Did you like our set?"
"You were shit!" he replied.

We discovered other creative ways to play badly: we appeared at Cambridge Corn Exchange higher up the bill than a newly-formed *Katrina and the Waves*. I think we played as well as could be expected, and gave a good account of ourselves, but following a band who were to have a future top ten single and win the Eurovision Song Contest is never going to cast you in a good light. We almost felt like apologising to the audience before we started playing.

By contrast, we once went on stage rather drunk. We came off stage thinking we'd played an amazing gig; popular opinion was that we were awful. We never went on stage drunk again.

A welcome challenge came when we got invited to be the backing band for the Huntingdon Youth Theatre's production of Godspell. It took a lot of discipline and time rehearsing, but it was well worth it. Consensus was that we did an excellent job, and I got to do a few rock-goddess guitar solos. I loved the bit where Jesus breaths his last and I got to launch a screaming wail from my guitar at full blast. Everyone should get to be a rock goddess at least once in their life.

During our time with Godspell we got to know the cast really well. We met our new singer Gareth there and became good friends with Donna who played Mary Magdelene. Some years later I saw standup comedian Donna McPhail on television, and was struck by her striking similarity to my friend Donna whom I hadn't seen since university. Was she the same person? She'd changed her surname. She looked so much thinner. I then saw her on a panel quiz show, and they surprised her with a photo of her and Hugh Grant at the Edinburgh Festival Fringe, shortly after our time at university: that was the Donna I remembered. Youth theatre to BBC2 prime time: at least one of us made it to the big time.

I would have dearly loved to have pursued a musical career after university. I auditioned for several bands around London but it was too competitive. Eventually I had to sell most of my gear to pay for my surgery. I've recently returned to music and now produce electronic dance music. Maybe it's still not too late to make it as an ageing muso?

In amongst all the gigs and parties, I did manage to find some time to study, and managed to leave university with a Master of Arts in mathematics. It was enough to get me a good job at the Ministry of Defence, and so keep me on track to my ultimate goal. I knew I was unlikely to be funded Gender Confirmation Surgery on the National Health Service, and so knew that I had to get some money behind me. I also felt I'd found the perfect job to transition in. Mission accomplished!

# Norway

The stories in this book all illustrate an aspect of trans life. Being trans is so fundamental to one's existence, it's hard not to bring it into any story one tells about one's life. This story is different. This is not a trans story.

It's September 1991 and I'm leading a slalom race at the Windsurfing World Championships in Stavanger, Norway. Does life get any better than this? This is amazing and a little bit scary. God I'm nervous.

Let's rewind eleven days though. There are a few adventures to get through yet.

It's two weekends previous and I'm at the British National Windsurfing Championships in Hastings. I have a hectic month ahead with business trips and the next round of the nationals in Troon, but sandwiched in the middle of it is the focus of my year: the World Championships. Tomorrow I drive up to Newcastle to catch the ferry across to Norway. After a few days settling in, we have a week of world championship competition. I'm hopeful of a good result.

I was on extremely good form. I'd been on the water training all year, whenever it was windy. I'd even got up early to go windsurfing before work if it was windy. Any non-windsurfing mornings before work were spent in the gym doing weights and cardio. Thinking back to this régime now, how did I ever manage to keep that up? The energy of youth!

So here I am standing on the beach at Hastings, with my race board and largest race sail hoisted above my head. The race board is long and cumbersome. The guys had always been amazed at how I could lift everything above my head as if it's a small wave board and sail, but it's just a matter of technique: you just get the balance right, put your head under the balance point, bend the knees, and using your lower body, lift. The guys can often get away with poor technique by using brute strength; I don't have that luxury.

I could do with a man's strength though: I'm looking at a vicious shore break. There's quite a swell and it's high tide, resulting in waves that build to about four feet then dump violently as they hit the shore. It takes great timing to ensure you let the wave break, run into the water on the back of the wave, and jump on before the next wave arrives. The winds are light though which doesn't help, as there's very little power in the sail to pull you out of the water and onto the board.

I choose my moment, run in, drop the board on the back of the wave, but I'm too early. As the wave sucks back it's too shallow to jump on the board. I wade out, but now the next, even bigger, wave is about to break. It catches me and the sail full in the face. I'm knocked over and pummelled face down into the shingle with the sail on top of me. I feel the immense weight of the water pinning me down under the sail. For a brief moment I wonder if I'm in serious danger of drowning. I've had experiences of being held under by waves when I've been wavesailing in big surf, and it's not pleasant: your lungs bursting as you wait for the wave to allow you to surface and breath. In reality these are usually short lived events, but they seem to last forever, as you try to escape your white-water tomb. It's what surfers call going through the rinse cycle. They don't have sails to worry about though!

Soon my ordeal is over as the weight of the water bursts the sail around me and I can stand up in the middle of my rig. I grab everything and drag it up onto the beach. I sit down hugging my knees to my chest, exhausted by my brief exertion. I have grit pebble-dashed to my forehead. I pick out all the pieces. I can't detect any blood, but I'd later realise I have a very unattractive rash across my forehead. Human bodies heal, sails don't. My most used race sail, the largest legal size allowed, for use in the minimum force 3-4 race conditions, is lying in tatters on the beach. Tomorrow I am driving off to Norway and I don't have my main race sail.

After an initial panic, I have a plan. I manage to get the home phone number of my sail sponsor from one of the other competitors. I run to the phone-box, wishing someone would invent a mobile phone, and my luck is in: he's at home. He has a replacement sail, and some sail numbers; we have to have our number on all our sails, and the numbers won't peel off one sail to stick on another. The plan is that he will get the sail to Fiona, my team mate, who will bring the sail over to Norway by air. She is travelling later in the week, as she can only get a week off work. Meanwhile I will take all of Fiona's kit and trailer with me by road, pick up all of Jo's kit on the way, and get myself by ferry to Norway. Jo and Fiona will then join me on the Friday in Norway, their kit waiting for them: the UK women's team thus complete and fully kitted out.

An overnight stay at Fiona's, and I'm on my way to the ferry port in Newcastle with Fiona's trailer attached. Jo rather conveniently lives in Newcastle. I meet Jo and we go shopping for a week's worth of food to stock the self catering chalet we've booked. This then becomes a crazy chase around local shops looking for suet. Apparently you can't have soup or stew without dumplings. I never knew this, I have to admit!

We swap cars, as Jo has a larger car and there's no way we can get three international competitors' kit in just one car and trailer. I leave Jo's and head to the ferry port.

Clang! Clatter! Clank!

Is anything going to go smoothly this week? The exhaust has just dropped off Jo's car! Why do windsurfers always have such an amazing array of kit, and such awful cars? I head back to Jo's realising that time is tight and the only option is to swap cars. Fortunately, her girlfriend's car is a similar size to hers, so we don't have to swap back to my small rusty Ford Escort. I'm soon on my way back to the ferry port, wondering whether, despite Jo's assurances, I am actually insured to drive the car I'm in. I get to the ferry in time, much to the relief of my frayed nerves. I do tend to get wound up in situations like this. I wish I could relax in stressful situations!

The ferry crossing was, shall we say, entertaining. I have never encountered seas so rough. There was a storm raging that rose to force 10 by the time we arrived in Norway. Fortunately the winds were behind us, and the ferry was huge, so was relatively stable. The German team had it far worse: they crossed from Denmark, with the wind and waves side-on to the boat. The German world champion was violently sick during the crossing, and she arrived looking extremely ill. I gained some comfort that even the queen of the waves could fall foul of a sea swell like that.

We had rented a wooden chalet in the holiday park overlooking the bay where we would be sailing. The scenery was beautiful, but the black shale surface of the park and trails around the bay reminded me of Welsh slate quarries, which always struck me as scars on an otherwise idyllic landscape. When the sun shone though, it picked out the golden sand of the bay, and it looked just stunning.

The next few days were spent checking my gear, and getting to know some of the other competitors. I got to know one of the French team, who was world champion in another branch of windsurfing. She invited me for a morning run around the bay. She really showed up my lack of running fitness! My cardio was good, but had mostly been done in the gym. I was in the presence of an elite sportswoman and I felt I'd just lost the first battle. I reminded myself that it's what happens on the water that counts. In the psychology battle though it was France 1, UK 0. She became a good friend though. My boyfriend was most impressed when I later received a postcard from a world champion!

There was a poignant moment the next day when a letter was posted outside the race organiser's office. It was from the Croatian team. The war in the former Yugoslavia was raging at that time, and Croatia were struggling to have their independence recognised. The windsurfing team were unable to leave the country. The letter described the conditions they were living in, and their regrets that they were unable to attend the championships. They asked that they be remembered and that we support their struggle for recognition of the independence of Croatia. It was very moving.

The day before the start of competition, Jo and Fiona arrived from the airport, to be reunited with their gear. Fiona brought my new sail with her, and to my relief, my sponsor had remembered to include a set of sail numbers. We were ready!

The competition is under way, and I'm on the start line of the first race. This is a course race and we are using long boards designed to get upwind quickly. I have my brand new sail and everything seems to be working fine. The setting is spectacular: I feel so small in the middle of the large bay, framed by the rocky coastline. The sun is trying to make an appearance but is losing out in the stormy skies. The dark clouds over the horizon have turned the sea an inky black, which makes the white horses stand out brilliant white. We are a fleet sailing in monochrome: a convoy at sea in an old war movie.

The gun goes and we are off, tacking up the bay to the windward mark a mile away. The fleet splits, as tactics come into play. I've lost sight of Jo, and assume she has headed out to sea. Fiona has headed in towards the bay. Do I stay on this tack and head in with Fiona, or do I tack and head out to sea? My instinct is to head out into open water where the wind will be stronger. I know that Fiona is very good at reading windshifts and wonder if she's gambling on the wind being pulled around the headland and giving us a lift. I decide to follow Fiona.

That was my first mistake of the championships, and all because I didn't follow my own instincts. I really should have trusted my own ability. The half of the fleet that had headed out to sea reached the windward mark first, leaving the rest of us to play catch up. I did claw some places back, and finished ahead of Fiona, but my middling position in the fleet of fifty sailors was not a reflection of my true capability. I needed to learn to listen to my own tactical advice!

When Jim Drake and Hoyle Schweitzer developed the original Windsurfer in 1970, it was a long voluminous board with a centreboard, or daggerboard, to aid in sailing upwind. As the wind picked up and the board started to plane, or skim over the surface of the water, the daggerboard became a liability, as the forces on it would try to flip the board over. On the original boards, it became traditional to pull the daggerboard out and sling it over one's shoulder when sailing off the wind. Later designs refined this so that the daggerboard was slender and pivoted, and could be retracted into the board by pushing its handle forward with your foot. As sails became more stable in design, and able to cope with stronger winds, a new breed of board emerged that was only intended for strong winds: these were low volume, short, highly manoeuvrable, and intended for winds of force four and above. These new boards had no daggerboard, just a fin at the back. They were intended for sailing across the wind; they were fast off the wind but tricky and slow to sail upwind. They were fun! These were the boards the recreational sailor aspired to. These were the sports cars of the windsurfing world.

The racing back then was split across two disciplines: course racing and slalom. The course racing was on long voluminous boards with daggerboards. The courses had an upwind leg of between one and two miles, followed by an M-shaped series of four offwind legs to get you back to the start, for the second of the two laps. The slalom discipline used short low-volume boards with no daggerboards. Courses were either figure of eight across the wind between two buoys, or were downwind courses, like a squashed version of the downwind part of the course race, with between four and eight legs. Slalom races were fast, often over thirty knots, and exciting: the carnage as eight sailors all tried to gybe around the same buoy was a spectacle in itself, despite this being a strictly no contact sport.

In 1991, change was in the air. The dividing line between longboards for course racing and short boards for slalom, was starting to blur. New super-fast sharp-edged slalom boards were coming on to the market. The sharp edges made them fast but less forgiving of poor technique. The sharp edges also made them go upwind better. Put a large fin on the back of the board, and in strong winds these were a match for the traditional longboards. The slalom boards couldn't sail as close to the wind as a longboard could, but their much greater speed meant that their upwind progress was faster. As boards developed through the 90s, the *course-slalom* board became dominant, and could beat the longboard in anything but the lightest of winds. The state of the art in 1991 at the Norway World Championships was that in force four the longboards were still dominant, in force five some sailors would be course racing on slalom boards, and in force six and above the entire fleet would be on slalom boards.

Back to the racing, and it's the next day and conditions have changed dramatically. The wind has shifted onshore and strengthened considerably. There is a very large swell rolling in, but the gently shelving beach means the breaking waves are easy to cope with. It's force six and I select a mid-sized rig from the quiver of sails I have rigged on the beach, and plug it into my slalom board. I fit a beautifully hand-crafted carbon-fibre blade fin to the back of the board: it's true state of the art from a specialist back home. Looking at the off-the-shelf designs around the beach, maybe this is my secret weapon. The racing today will be very different!

The gun goes and I'm in my element: these are the conditions I relish. Whenever the conditions permit at home, this is what I enjoy doing most: playing in the waves only half a mile from my doorstep. What magnificent waves we have here today! These are waves to be tamed not played with though. Although getting airborne is at times unavoidable, today we are racing and must stay grounded. The ground here though is great grey corridors of water, like a giant corrugated iron roof with us tiny creatures trying to pop over each corrugation as it tries to force us downwind. The spectators on the shore lose sight of us between the waves, only seeing us pop up as we try to get over each crest, such is the height of the swell.

The wind is strong, but I have the perfect five-square-metre sail for the conditions: I'm just on the edge of control but still powered up when in the lulls between the waves. I try to use the full width of the bay, to minimise the number of times I need to tack: a drawback of using a slalom board like this is that it almost sinks when at a standstill, making tacking, or turning it into the wind, a tricky affair. I tack, and as I feared, I over balance and drop back into the water. I am still holding on though, and I quickly waterstart[7] back onto the board, barely a hair wet[8]. Another tack, this time with better technique, and I'm heading towards the windward mark.

It's hard to describe the elation I felt as I rounded the windward mark: there were only two sailors ahead of me! Amongst the best women windsurfers in the world I was in third place. I knew I was in good form but I never expected this. This was a completely new type of racing: using slalom boards for course racing. It needed the very best technique. It needed an exceptional feel for the wind and the waves, and how to get the most from the combination of those elements. I had what it took and was beating all but two of the very best in the world.

*Focus girl, don't lose it, there's still a lap and a half to go.*

I look around for the next mark but I can't see it. I pick a line off-wind and try to make out the buoy in the distance. The organisers had chosen to use small round solid buoys with flags on top, rather than the usual giant

---

[7] Many people may have an image of holiday-makers standing on a board hauling the sail out of the water. In strong winds though, experts employ the waterstart: the power of the wind in the sail is used to pull the sail, with sailor hanging on underneath, out of the water and pull the sailor gracefully onto the board.

[8] It's actually a total immersion sport in thick wetsuits. In these conditions you have a continuous spray of water hitting you in the face.

inflatable buoys. The problem with flags is that they align with the wind: you can't see them from upwind!

A slalom board relies on the fact that it's planing: skimming over the surface rather than ploughing through the water. It needs power derived from the wing-like shape of the sail to achieve this. They can't sail directly downwind however, as the sail would simply be acting like a bag, a spinnaker, and not generating any aerodynamic lift. As you bear away from the wind there comes a point when you are no longer generating enough power and the board drops off the plane and starts to wallow. A feature of very strong winds is that there's no shortage of power in the sail and the angles you are able to achieve into and away from the wind are quite extreme. I had been sailing a course which I thought was slightly off the wind and heading to the first of the downwind buoys, but in fact I was heading almost straight downwind towards the finish line!

My race is going well, and I'm making good progress towards the next buoy, but I soon realise that the two competitors ahead of me are nowhere to be seen. I look around. They are upwind of me. What's going on? I then spot the buoy they are heading towards, and realise my mistake.
*Aagh! You idiot!*
I head upwind and realise I'm on a very tight upwind angle to make the buoy. Will I need to tack? This is slowing me down dramatically, and I'm being caught by the others. The leader gybes round the buoy followed by number two. It's starting to look like I will make the buoy without tacking, as I pinch into the wind. Number three gybes, followed by four......five... I've made it! I'm in sixth place. It's not the best gybe, but I didn't have much speed into the buoy. I'm now slotted back into the fleet as we file down the course.

I was hoping that I'd make up places on the next lap, but it wasn't to be. I crossed the line in sixth place: my best ever position in a world championship course race. What might have been without my shortsightedness?

The racing continued in very rough seas, and some solid results followed. One of the men had equipment failure in their race and ended up on the rocks pounded by the surf. He was taken to hospital with broken ribs. These are the dangers of windsurfing in these conditions; we accept them as part of the extreme nature of the sport. I had never anticipated one of the unseen dangers of the sport though; what followed taught me a valuable lesson.

We had been racing all day. I'd had a cereal bar or two for energy, but we hadn't really had a break for lunch and I hadn't eaten enough. I also probably had not had enough to drink, having spent much of the day on the water: there's no stowage on a windsurfer. Naturally I was tired. I looked at my beautifully decorated slalom board on the beach and just wanted to curl up on it and go to sleep. I did just that. I curled up on it, but as I waited to drift away into oblivion, a small voice deep inside me called me back. Something told me this was not a sensible course of action. I mustered what energy I could, stowed my sail rigs, and got into the car with the other girls.

I sat in the passenger seat and shut my eyes. The girls were talking to me, but I didn't want to listen. I was only half aware of what they were saying. I felt very antisocial. I felt miserable. I wish they'd just leave me alone and let me sleep. *World, go away!*

At the chalet, I was in zombie mode, only half reacting to the world around me. Through the haze someone suggested I should go shower. *Yes, shower, that seems like a sensible move.* I stepped into the shower in my wetsuit, and peeled it off under the lovely hot crystal spray. Wetsuit and body now clean and salt free, I towelled off and reality started to creep back in: I was cold. I was very cold.

I shuffled back into the chalet, refused the mug of hot chocolate being pushed at me and went to bed to get warm. I lay there fully clothed under a thick duvet, and felt chilled to the core. I waited for the warmth; it didn't come. I felt miserable. I was in despair. I buried my head in the pillow and burst into tears. I cried my heart out. Never in my life have I experienced such misery. I wanted the world to end.

My friends had now figured that maybe I wasn't my usual bubbly self. I now accepted the hot chocolate, and felt really nauseous. They forced me to drink. Another hot chocolate followed and the nausea increased. I was being offered stew but I really didn't want it. I wished they'd just leave me alone. I tried a forkful. Another. As I ate, the world started to feel like a better place. The nausea was retreating. I was starting to feel warmer. I was starting to feel better. With each forkful I took a step back from that dark place. By the end of the meal, I felt shaken but recovered.

Dehydration, hunger, low blood sugar, exhaustion and cold had allowed my core temperature to drop to dangerous levels: all my fault and entirely preventable. I will never again suffer from hypothermia.

I learnt another lesson too: stew tastes really good with suet dumplings!

The next day dawned, the wind had swung cross-shore once more, and it was time for slalom. The course would be a figure of eight between two buoys positioned across the wind: one near the beach and the other out at sea. The start would be a beach start: we would all line up on the beach with our boards and sails held aloft and run into the surf on the signal. This was not an ideal way to start a world championship slalom heat, as there was luck involved in getting the upwind starting position, but it was good for the spectators.

This feels good. I've had a great draw and I'm one down from the windward start position: only one sailor who can steal my wind. It's brilliantly sunny, which lifts my mood. The sea is flat compared to yesterday, and the menacing black and grey has been replaced with welcoming blues and greens, interlaced with brilliant white ponies.

The gun goes and we run headlong into the shallows. Maybe I'm not such a bad runner after all as I get ahead of my windward rival into clean air. I have to judge the right moment to launch: too soon and the fin will catch, too late and I'll lose time. I'm now up to my knees and running is becoming tricky. I drop the board flat on the water, grab the boom with both hands, jump straight on, and try to hang all my weight through the boom and down though the mast. It's tricky to control the power in the sail when committing all your weight through it. I judge it perfectly and the board starts to plane immediately and reaches top speed quickly. I pop my feet in the straps, hook in to the harness, and sail off ahead of the fleet.

I sail off ahead of the fleet!

I'm leading a world class fleet of windsurfers down a World Championship slalom course.

I'm soon at the first buoy. I sheet the sail in to control the power, lean in to initiate the turn, and the board carves a perfect arc close to the buoy. I flip the sail on the new tack, step forward to balance the board, sheet in to get the power back on, step into the straps, hook in, and away we go: a perfect gybe with almost no loss of speed. I extend my lead and head back to the beach. Another gybe, and I'm heading back out to sea, with a comfortable lead.

*This is amazing. I'm leading a World Championship slalom race. I only have one more gybe. Please don't get this wrong. Don't mess this up. God this is scary.*

Windsurfing is an extremely technical sport. To be able to carve gybe a board in a choppy sea and gusty winds at a precise arc, requires not just technique, but relaxation. Your knees are the shock absorbers. Stiffen up and the board no longer tracks smoothly: it has a tendency to bounce out of the turn.

I head towards the last mark. I'm tense. Psychology has never been a strong point and once again I'm talking myself out of this. *Don't fall. Don't fail.*

I initiate the turn with stiff straight legs. As the board hits the apex it skips out of the turn and almost stops. I flip the sail and grab the boom on the other side. With the drop in speed I now have the full force of the wind in the sail. I'm pulled off balance and have to let go with my right hand to kill the power. The board is starting to sink. I pull the sail back towards me as the board turns into the wind. I have control of the sail now, and with another big wobble, I power up the sail and bear the board away, the rest of the fleet bearing down on me. I get the board back on the plane, hook in, and I'm off again on the last reach of the race. I'm still in the lead.

I cross the finish line at full speed. I spot a little bit of chop that looks like a suitable ramp, kick the board up into the wind and pop a nice little victory jump over the finish line. I've won a heat of the World Championships! I'm through to the semi finals!

Sadly I wasn't so fortunate in the semis, but I placed well in the losers' final. Nerves again played their part, and I wasn't so lucky with start positions. It was a good solid performance though.

At the end of the week's competition I was rewarded with 14th place, and the highest placed British female. It's rare the press report on women's windsurfing, but my efforts were rewarded with a picture in a national magazine and the caption:
"Anne Cognito: Occasional flashes of brilliance".

# Coming out

Coming out as gay isn't easy. There is terrible homophobia in the world still, and coming out stories abound with tales of heroism and courage to be oneself in the face of social pressure. We live in the twenty first century though and things are so much better than in the 80s. Trans people aren't so lucky: we still live in the 80s as far as society's attitudes are concerned. Coming out as gay is pretty straightforward compared to the perils of coming out as trans.

I've experienced coming out from two very different perspectives: before transition and after transition. I'm fortunate that I rarely get clocked as trans and am able to lead a stealth life, such that there are people who've known me twenty five years who have no idea I'm trans; coming out to them can be just as traumatic as it would have been pre-transition, and it really shouldn't be. Both these types of coming out can be frankly terrifying, with a fear of the unknown and of the possible rejection by people you love, but there is a third type of coming out, and my first experience of it was delicious fun. It went like this:

It's the summer of 1985, a few months after transition, and I'm visiting my best friend Tina at her flat in North London. Tina and I were at university together, and she is to-date my most successful coming out experience. My coming out to her was such a non-event that I honestly cannot remember when I told her. She was so completely at ease with the news of my impending transition that I have no recollection of telling her, unlike other disastrous comings out that have seared themselves into my memory.

The details of this summer's day however, have etched themselves into my memory for entirely different reasons. I remember them so clearly. I even remember exactly what I was wearing: pastel yellow skin tight jeans and a beige cotton knit batwing top. My hair was a typical 80s light brown bubble perm, these being the days when I permed rather than coloured my hair. I've always had to treat my hair in some fashion, never having been able to accept my plain brown straight-as-can-be hair.

Tina and I are sitting chatting and sharing a cup of tea. We're talking about our jobs: her work at a children's book publisher, and my newly assigned work analysing torpedo test data. It's just your average day, and I'd just popped round for a chat.

There's a knock at the door, and Tina goes to answer it. A moment later she rushes in with a look of panic on her face.
"It's Stephen! Are you ok with this?"
Stephen is our mutual friend from university. We both know Stephen extremely well, but Stephen is unaware that I'm trans and have transitioned. I figure now is as good a time as any to break the news to him, so I quickly nod my approval to Tina. I don't really have much choice in the matter anyway as Stephen is close behind Tina and has now entered the room.
"Stephen, this is Anne."
"Hi Stephen."
"Anne."
As is typical of his style, he offers his hand, I offer mine, and he gently shakes my hand by the tips of my fingers.

I'm rather taken aback by the events unfolding. Tina is chatting with Stephen catching up with each other's news, and every now and then Tina glances at me with a glint in her eye.

*Stephen has no idea who I am!*

Tina is having a hard time holding back. By the magic of body language we've established that I'm ok with what she's about to do, so Tina eventually cuts into the conversation with:
"You don't know who this is, do you?"
Stephen's looking puzzled.
"She was at university with us."
There's a blank look on his face.
"She was at our college."
That really provokes a reaction from Stephen. He's the kind of guy who would pride himself on knowing every woman in our year. As if to answer Stephen's unvoiced question, Tina continues:
"She was in our year."
Stephen's puzzled look deepens. That's really thrown him.
"She was in the band The Innocent Bystanders."
I can almost see Stephen's thought process:

*I remember the band but she's not the backing singer.*
"She played guitar."
Tina has delivered the punchline, but amazingly Stephen is still puzzled.
*They never had a female guitarist, and I thought I went to all their gigs.*
Tina is as amazed as me. I guess the brain can't cope with a switch from male to female when it comes to facial recognition, even though my face was largely the same as it always had been: I was too skinny for it to have rounded out to any great extent, but I guess the hormones must have made some difference.
Tina switches from the band theme, to go in with what must surely be the final clue:
"She had the room next to you in the first year."

I wish I could experience that moment again and again, but it's something of a one time deal. People often use the term *jaw dropping* where such hyperbole is quite unwarranted, but here it was a very literal description: I don't think I'd ever witnessed someone's jaw drop in quite that fashion. The look on Stephen's face was quite incredible. We'd had him sitting through the clues in silence, and his silence continued: quite something for someone as normally eloquent as Stephen. After what seemed an eternity, Stephen finally managed:
"Er...hi!"

I never really managed to gauge his reaction to my news, as he still seemed in a state of shock when he left, but I think he was cool with it. It's always hard to gauge people's reactions, as unless they are my parents, they are unlikely to direct transphobic slurs straight at my face. I haven't seen anything of him since, but I haven't made any effort to keep in contact with him.

I wonder if Stephen is a gossipmonger?

# Rhodes

This should have been another non-trans-related story. Unfortunately it isn't.

It's 1992 and I am the only woman representing the UK at the World Windsurfing Championships on the island of Rhodes.

I have many amazing memories of the championships, but they are overshadowed by one event: a transphobic assault.

We had some downtime from the competition and I went with my boyfriend Dougie, who at that time didn't know I'm trans, to explore the old town of Rhodes. The medieval citadel of Rhodes is beautiful. It's amazingly well preserved. It dates back to the Knights Templar in the fourteenth century. The ancient streets have such a wonderful atmosphere. It's a great antidote to the beach-centred holiday vibe of where we were staying, and a great way to switch off and relax from the stresses of competition.

Naturally it was hot, and I was wearing minimal clothing typical of all the other women wandering along the Avenue of the Knights that afternoon. I was in shorts, Reef sandals and a vest top. I was showing plenty of flesh, but no different to anyone else. I was walking along with Dougie without a care in the world. We weren't holding hands; we had an intimate relationship but we weren't that touchy-feely, at least not in public.

What happened next almost seems funny looking back, but at the time was quite scary.

I was attacked with a Bible.

I was vaguely aware of a guy preaching at the corner of the street. I always ignore them. They're happy doing their thing, but to be honest they strike me as a little bit odd. I'm not into religion, and don't like being preached at. They can do their thing, and I'll do mine.

As we approached, he saw me, and his attitude instantly changed. I'd say I was 'clocked' by him. I always know when someone has that look. I'd suddenly gone from just another woman on the street, minding her own business, to an object of hate. I've never been able to understand what it is about me that can flick a switch in some people and generate such hatred. Do tall masculine-looking cis women have similar problems with the fringe element of society? Does my trans history shine like a beacon for only the haters to see?

He rushed from his corner spot in the shadows and ran straight at me brandishing his Bible. It was frankly terrifying. He was babbling nonsense, but I got the gist of what he was saying: I was eternally damned, and basically God and the rest of humanity hated me. What a lovely man!

Was he about to beat me up with his Bible, or was he going to use it as a force for good and cast out my demons?

Fortunately I didn't have to find out the answer the hard way: Dougie was ex-parachute-regiment - the hard boys of the British Army.

I was most impressed! Dougie went into action and took control. He didn't have to get too physical with the guy: he just asserted his presence, putting himself between the preacher and me. Dougie is not the biggest of guys, but it was impressive to watch how he dominated the guy. I really hope it scared the preacher to the extent he had scared me.

It was a great feeling having someone to protect you: someone who would put himself in the way of danger for you without a moment's hesitation. I'd never experienced that before. As scary as the attack was, it was lovely to feel protected and cared for. We had a very nice time together that evening.

I wondered if Dougie had questioned the guys motives for the attack. He probably just thought he was a weirdo who took exception to women exposing too much flesh. I knew the reason for the attack though and it brought all the old insecurities back. The next day I was going to have to face the best windsurfers in the world. Now was not the time for self doubt.

If I had any doubts about myself then the events of the following day certainly didn't show it!

The wind had finally arrived and the opening course race of the championship was scheduled in a perfectly side-shore force four. The course was laid out with the windward mark directly opposite the main area on the beach, giving a perfect vantage point for the spectators and the male competitors cheering us on while they waited for their race.

The advances in board design meant that despite the relatively light wind, some of the women, mainly the lighter ones, were on the new breed of short course-slalom boards. I had to go with my traditional long board with its daggerboard, knowing that there wasn't quite enough wind to propel my extra weight on the smaller board. I would have an advantage upwind, but I'd most likely lose out in speed off the wind.

It was a crowded start with over fifty competitors trying to out-manoeuvre each other and get an advantageous position ahead of the gun. As is common in many sailing races, the line of boards, stretching between the committee boat at one end and the buoy at the other, had bowed. This is quite common when the sailors in the middle of the line can't see either end of the line and can only rely on the positions of the other boards around them. The boards in the middle end up quite a way back from the line.

I was aware that the line had bowed, but I had my own techniques to avoid it. I had taken what's called a *transit* before the start. By positioning myself the other side of the committee boat before the start, I had been able to sight along the line and had spotted a tree on the land that was in line with buoy and boat. You have to be careful buoy and boat are stationary and not dragging their anchors, so I'd rechecked a few minutes later and all was well. I then knew that as long as I could see the buoy to the right of the tree, then I was behind the line.

I sailed forward from the line of boards until I had a clear view of the end buoy, and realised we were all quite a way back from the line. I continued to sail forward until tree and buoy were almost in line and held my position waiting for the gun: textbook technique.

I could hear shouting from behind me:
"You're over the line!"
Did they really believe that or were they playing mind games? Taking a transit is such a basic bit of race-craft that it surprised me no one else was

joining me, given the high standard of sailors present. Unlike Norway where I regretted following Fiona, this time I had confidence in my own judgement and held my ground.

The gun went and I was away on my own in clear wind. I didn't need to worry what others were doing; I already had an advantage and could concentrate on picking my own line to the windward mark and getting the best out of the board.

At the windward mark I was still in the lead. I led the world championship fleet around the buoy. It was a great moment. I could hear the British guys cheering from the beach. It felt wonderful.

It wasn't to last though. As I suspected, the shorter course-slalom boards had a speed advantage on the reaches and by the first downwind buoy I had already been overtaken by the reigning world champion. I held on though on the next lap and got a top ten finish. It was a good start to the campaign.

I had another good championships. I could tell you about the astonishing fifty knots of steady wind they made us race in, while the men complained to the organisers that it wasn't safe to send the men out, let alone the women. I could tell you about the slalom beach start where I hadn't realised I'd been positioned in front of a concrete World War Two landing-craft trap, breaking my fin and almost my knee cap on it. I could tell you about being one of only two finishers in the fifty-knot-wind losers' final, the other being a six-feet-one-inch German woman. I could tell you about me being adopted by the German team as I was the only UK woman and I sailed for a German manufacturer. I could tell you that for the second year running I finished fourteenth in the world.

I could tell you all these things, but the Rhodes World Windsurfing Championships will always be remembered for being attacked with a Bible.

## Coolest student ever

*June 1983*

It's the end of the last term of my last year of university. I'm sitting in the great hall at an oak banqueting table having lunch. Imagine the lavishness of Hogwarts, but without the floating candles and sky views. I'm sitting with my back to the oak wainscoting. Above me an old master of the college looks down from his canvas, gazing out approvingly at the achievements of his students. You can imagine the paintings on the walls all animated in Harry Potter style, nodding in approval at another batch of students, glorying in their achievements, their hard work behind them. This isn't Hollywood though, this is the genuine article; you can literally smell the five hundred years of history running through the place. Just what is that smell? I guess I've got used to it.

We are brought back to the modern world by our student uniform of jeans and T shirt, and the plastic dinner trays in front of us. Evening formal dinners have a dress code: we are required to wear our undergraduate gowns. This is lunch though, and the casual attire and self-serve cafeteria fare jar slightly with the formal ambience of the hall.

I'm seated with a small group of friends. We've mostly finished eating and we're chatting away, passing the time of day; we're in no hurry, our studying is done. My friends opposite me get up and leave and we continue to chat amongst ourselves in our group of five. I look up and catch the eye of Jane as she walks in with a male friend. They sit down opposite me, with Jane diagonally to my left, and her friend directly opposite me.

I hardly notice the atmosphere change as they sit down. I guess the group dynamic always changes when new people are added. I'm relaxed and carefree and easily incorporate the stranger into our group.

It transpires that Jane is showing our guest around the college. If we had a head girl then Jane would be her. It's hard to fathom how someone emerges as a leader in a group of people that requires no leader but Jane fits the bill: maybe it's her air of authority, her political activity or her social privilege.

Whatever the reasons, if you needed someone to show a guest around the college, then Jane was the person for the job.

Jane hasn't introduced her guest, but I engage him in conversation, and include him seamlessly into the general chat. The others seem to have clammed up a bit, but maybe they don't have my stamina: I can talk for England.

I would like to include the dialogue between myself and our guest. I can't. It was fleeting and inconsequential. I simply don't remember. Maybe it went something like this:
"So Jane's showing you around?"
"Yes"
"Do you like what you see?"
"I do. It seems a really good place to study."
"Well it's certainly quiet. We don't get so many tourists, as we're not on The Backs."
"The food seems good."
"The food is great, and the formal halls are really cheap at just one pound, so well worth going to, despite having to wear your gown, and you can save money at lunch time if you want by just having a pasty in the bar, and they use the college crockery with gold leaf around the edge so it sparks in the microwave, ooh, and the bar is really cheap, they have special nights with promos when they get a barrel or two in, but if you really want cheap drinks then you have to join the Campaign for Real Gin, they have just the best parties ever, and there are parties all the time here, depending on what subject you're doing you get all the studying out of the way during the day and then your evenings are just one long party, and you can get into other colleges too, but you might need to keep a low profile, but generally people turn a blind eye, as discounted food and drink are meant to be just for the students of the particular college, but Newnham is great for lunch, and Magdalene does great dinners, and you need to check out the music scene too, we get some really good bands, and the student bands are always good too...."

I have no idea what I said, but it was probably along those lines, with me doing my usual scatty stream of consciousness. Whatever it was I said, it was just idle chat, with me extolling the virtues of the college I loved. I do remember the odd reaction of the others though, and how I seemed to dominate the conversation with everyone else as mere onlookers.

Lunch and conversation over, Jane and her guest thanked us, and left us chatting and passing the time of day. As they disappeared through the doors, a hush descended on our group. All eyes were on me. I looked around at the shocked faces and let out a surprised "What?"
"You do know who that was, don't you?"
"The guy with Jane?"
"Yes"
"Errrrrr......no?"
"That was Prince Edward!"

In my defence, I do know who the members of the royal family are, and in a family group would be able to name all of them. However, when a casually attired member of the royal family walks over to sit opposite you and engage in conversation, without entourage, it doesn't immediately occur to you that you are talking to the third in line to the throne. Was I being dim? Maybe. Was I acting without airs and graces and treating our guest like he was just a regular guy? Definitely.

Prince Edward chose my college to study at the following year. I may have been the gossip of the college bar that evening, but I'd like to think I had a hand in Prince Edward's decision. I left him thinking the students at my college were the most down to earth people, totally unphased by the presence of royalty. I was just the coolest student ever.

# Support

It's tough being trans. We need support from our friends and family. These days attitudes to trans people are changing and families are more supporting than ever, but that support is by no means certain, and transition often splits families apart. It's then that we rely on support from within the trans community. Fortunately, these days, that support is just a few keystrokes away, out there on the Internet.

Its hard to imagine where we'd be without the Internet. Type 'transsexual' into Google and if you can get past the porn sites then you have a wealth of information at your fingertips. I unfortunately can imagine what it would be like without the Internet as I transitioned in the 80s: I transitioned in a world without Twitter, without Facebook and most critically without Google. I did have a search engine though: it was called *The Phone Book*.

I was so nervous picking up the phone and seeking help. It felt like I was confessing deep dark sins. I'd found the number for the *Gay and Lesbian Switchboard*, an information line run from London; they gave me the number of the *TV/TS Support Group*, also in London.

In my last year of university I started making regular trips to London to visit the support group. I'd managed to get a small wardrobe together. I remember my very first outfit: I had a pink and purple gypsy skirt with silver detailing, quite voluminous and very feminine; I wore it with an Indian cotton blouse with some nice embroidery. I bought both items on Cambridge market; they looked quite good considering how cheap they were. I was lucky getting the size right for my clothes, but the shoes I was going to have to try on. I took a size nine, and needed to go to a shop catering for larger sizes. I worried about being spotted if I tried to source the shoes in Cambridge, so I took a trip to London's Oxford Street to buy the shoes, such was my paranoia.

I was so nervous scouting out where to buy the shoes. It felt like I was about to out myself publicly. First I had to find a shop that sold size nines; fortunately this wasn't difficult as I spotted a *Tall and Small* sign in the

window of Saxone. Downstairs I found their shelf of larger sizes, and there was a pair of pink court shoes with a medium heel that seemed exactly what I was looking for. I paced around the store for a while, but there was no putting this off any longer; I found the nearest assistant and nervously, but I hoped calmly, said:
"Can I have these in a size nine please?"
The assistant returned with the shoes, and just as I was wondering if I should grab them, pay, and run, she said:
"Are they for you?"
"Yes."
I was relieved. I didn't have to explain any further; she just opened the box, set them down and let me try them on. I think she could tell how nervous I was. They fitted quite well. I walked a couple of steps up and down, but was trying not to call attention to myself. It wasn't the first time I'd walked in heels, but it was a few years since I'd outgrown my mum's shoes. The assistant calmly packed up the shoes in their box, and handed them back to me to go and pay. She was so matter-of-fact and professional, much to my relief; I suspect she'd served a lot more trans customers than just me.

As much as I would have liked to have tried a wig on in a shop, that seemed just one step too far. Having hovered outside the wig section of several department stores, I'd never managed to pluck up the courage to go try one on. Eventually I ordered a wig from the back pages of one of the Sunday newspapers. I just hoped that when the item was placed in my pigeonhole in the college mail room it didn't have *This is a wig* printed on it. Two weeks later to my relief a plain package arrived containing my wig. It was a long curly dark brown affair; it wasn't the best wig, but I was a student and you get what you pay for. It would do. I had my underwear; I had my makeup; I now had all I needed for my first trip to the London support group.

On the platform of Cambridge station that Friday evening I bumped into one of my college friends. What if she asks where I'm going? What does she think is in my holdall? I can't believe how paranoid I was. I was seriously scared of being found out. Everything about how I'd been brought up, and how society views us, told me that I was some sort of pervert. I was about to cross the border into another world: another world of creeps, freaks, and weirdos.

I found the support group without much of a problem. They had their own premises in Islington. I walked nervously through the door and was immediately made to feel welcome by all the people there. My first impression on seeing everyone:

*Wow! They're all like me!*

There were cross dressers of all shapes and sizes. Everyone was so down to earth and relaxed; it wasn't the den of iniquity I'd feared. These were just normal people who shared something in common. Everyone presented as female: there were no trans men. These days it is accepted that there are as many transgender men as there are women, but back then it seemed that this was largely male to female, such was society's willingness to accept varying gender expression from women but not from men.

The organiser of the group was Yvonne, whom I'd spoken to on the phone. She showed me through to the back room where I could get changed. Some minutes later I reappeared in my outfit, curtsied politely, and joined the group, who were all very complimentary on my look. For the first time in my life I felt like I belonged; I felt normal.

I started attending the group regularly, when the band's gigging schedule would allow. When questioned about my trips to London, I'd just say I was visiting friends: essentially the truth. After a few more visits, I was admitted to the inner circle, and invited to have a meal at the Philbeach Hotel. The Philbeach was a hotel run by a gay couple, that catered for gay clientele, and was friendly towards cross dressers. It seemed like an adventure in itself, travelling across London in someone's car, and then parading into the hotel in our heels and finery. I enjoyed the meal and the general experience, but I started to see another side to the behaviour of some of my friends. Once outside the confines of the support group, their behaviour got a little coarse, exhibitionist, and dare I say *male*? I remember one of them being quite disrespectful to a waitress. I also remember one taking their rubber breast form out and bouncing it on the table. I was embarrassed.

At the end of the evening, in the car driving back across London, one of the girls turned to me and said:
"You want more than this, don't you?"

I looked perhaps a little puzzled by the question, so she qualified it: "You're transsexual aren't you?"

I'd naïvely assumed that everyone who wanted to dress like a woman would naturally want to be a woman, but I was realising this certainly wasn't the case. In getting to understand my own gender identity, I was realising that most of my new found friends identified as male, but liked to occasionally express a female side of their personality. I was beginning to understand the difference between, to use the parlance of the day, a transvestite and a transsexual. Having first thought that everyone in the room that day when I first arrived was like me, I now had the realisation:

*Wow! No one here is like me.*

The atmosphere seemed to change from that moment on. It was supposed to be a support group, but some of them seemed quite hostile to the idea of me transitioning. They tried to convince me that I should view this as a hobby. I was told that I wasn't transsexual and I'd ruin my life if I tried to transition. I'd gone from feeling I could talk about anything, to feeling there were things I shouldn't discuss. Once more I felt like an outsider, a freak.

There's a certain irony that my mum was convinced that having moved to London, I'd fallen in with the wrong crowd, and they were trying to persuade me to do things I didn't want to do; in fact the exact opposite was happening, much to my dismay.

I've seen these sort of divisions in more recent online communities. Maybe it's a feature of oppressed minority groups that some feel very protective of their little corner of the community. It may be that the London support group felt they were being protective of me: if it was tough for cross dressers then it was even tougher for transsexual folks. Whatever the reason behind their hostility, once I'd found another support group, the *Self Help Association For Transsexuals*, I never went back to the group.

*SHAFT* has to be the worst acronym ever for a trans support group, but they were good people. It was run by trans woman Judy Couzins, by way of a series of newsletters. After university I moved to London and got to know Judy quite well. She was trained in electrolysis, and I had several sessions with her, to remove what little facial hair I had. It was lucky I only had a small amount of growth either side of my chin; I hated electrolysis; it was so painful.

Until a few years ago, Judy was the only trans person I'd ever met, which perhaps gives you an idea of how isolating being trans was thirty years ago.

These days I'm on the other side of the support fence, my chosen platform being Twitter, under the hash tag #girlslikeus. There's a really vibrant community on Twitter, and it's really opened my eyes to how social media can be used well, and not as a platform for self-publicists, as had been my view of it previously.

There can still be some, shall we say, *lively*, debates on Twitter, but as a support network it functions really well. It's also opened my eyes to the lives of trans people around the world, and made me realise how much harder life is for trans people in other countries. By raising awareness of the injustices perpetrated against my brothers and sisters, I hope the Internet can be a real force for social change.

If you'd like to follow me on Twitter, I'm **@a_cognito**. Come say hi, don't be shy!

# Local glory

*1992-1993*

Despite my relative success in windsurfing on the national and international stages, the nicest recognition is always that which you receive at home.

I'd always been queen of my local beach. I was a face. Guys would come up to me to say hello to me by name. I was always embarrassed that, with a few exceptions, I knew no one's name. I've always been bad with names, and it never ceases to be a source of embarrassment.
"Good morning Anne, there're some nice clean waves out there."
"Hey morning um.... Yes, really good conditions."
To be fair, there were lots of them, but only one of me. There were just a few other girls who windsurfed at my beach, and I knew most of them by name, but there was only one who'd represented her country.

I remember one particular evening down at the beach. I knew conditions were going to be good, and I got there straight after work. It was windy, but the slight offshore nature of the wind meant the sea was fairly flat. I decided this was an evening for slalom practice. By my usual system of educated guesswork, a combination of sea state and standing at the water's edge facing into the wind, I rigged the appropriate sized sail and plugged it into my slalom board. I positioned my home made buoy - a spray painted gallon can attached to some thin cord, old chain and a purchased mini anchor - just off the beach, in sufficient depth of water to allow gybing with no fear of grounding the fin.

It may have been serious training, doing gybe after gybe after gybe, but it was really good fun. This never seemed to get boring. The joy of windsurfing is that conditions are never the same twice. Tonight may have been flat, but flat meant fast, and I'd felt on top form. I never fell in once. All my gybes were going well, and by the end of the session I was sailing out of the gybes almost as fast as I was going into them, the board never coming off the plane[9].

At the end of the session I sailed in, and with my usual style hoisted the board and sail over my head, balanced there using gravity and the power of the wind across the sail. I then calmly climbed the steps up the sea wall, board and sail aloft, and deposited my kit next to my car on the other side. I was just about to go back for the buoy when an old guy approached me.
"Are you Anne?"
"Yes"
"It's too windy for me tonight, so I sat in the car and watched you sailing. I'd just like to say thank you. It was a real pleasure watching you. That was an amazing display."

I was stunned. I thanked him and shook his hand.

The above tale is not a story of everyday trans folk. It's just a story of a woman getting recognition for something she happens to be good at. It meant so much to me. It's no exaggeration that the world can be exceptionally hostile when you are trans. You feel on your guard all the time waiting for the moment when someone decides you're 'other' and a worthy target. Hostility towards me started with my parents. I was denied the one source of love and affection which most people take for granted. To this day, compliments just feel so good. It's like I've been to hell and back just to get to the point where someone can turn to me and tell me that I've touched their life and they thank me for it. I'm sure trans people don't have the monopoly on emotional deprivation, but positive affirmation always feels so so good.

That same spot on the beach was the scene of two other moments which will stay with me forever.

---

[9] As previously described, in a moderate wind, windsurfers plane, that is to say they skim over the surface of the water at speed, rather than slowly ploughing through it like a ship.

Each year, my home town hosts a windsurfing festival. At its peak it attracted over 500 windsurfers. The sight of that many boards on the water was truly something to behold. This year it would attract 250 people, still quite a spectacle.

The Saturday would be a mass open sea course race: a dash along the coast for about three miles, gybe around a large navigation buoy, dash back, tack around another buoy, and then tack back up into the wind to finish on the beach between two flags. The wind was strong and offshore. The sea was fairly flat, but the further out to sea you went, the stronger the wind got, and the choppier the sea became.

I'd never witnessed a start like this. It was four times the size of anything I'd ever taken part in before. The start line stretched a mile out to sea. It seemed that all the pro sailors were out at sea by the committee boat, and the amateurs were in the calmer waters nearer shore.

The start of a sailing race isn't a simple get set, go. In our race there was a six minute warning gun, with another gun at one minute to go, and then a gun at the start. The start line is an imaginary line between the committee boat and a buoy, or in this case a large flag on the beach. At the start you must be behind the line. If you are over the line then you must return and recross it, but due to the size of this fleet, we were warned that there would be disqualifications. The start line was positioned so that we would be crossing it on the fastest point of sailing: a broad reach. The professional way to do this type of start is not to wait stationary behind the line but to use your skill and judgement and hit the line at full speed just as the gun goes.

My approach would be to hare off in the opposite direction with one minute to go and after thirty seconds gybe the board round, taking great care not to get it wrong and fall in, and head back to the start. I'd be watching the countdown on my watch mounted at the top of my left arm, judging my run in to the line. With skill and a little bit of luck I'd be close to the line but not over it when the gun went, and already moving at top speed.

The start that day went perfectly and immediately all the pro sailors were ahead of the rest of the fleet. I was already in the top thirty. The three mile reach seemed to fly by: we were probably doing close to thirty knots. It was a beautifully sunny day, as is often the case with northerly winds in the UK, and the brilliant white wakes and spray from the hundreds of boards, albeit with most of them behind me, looked spectacular.

We were soon at the buoy, and it was time to sort the men (and women) from the buoys. It's all very well being able to sail fast in a straight line using brute force and ignorance, but it takes skill and finesse to turn the board round in high winds. There was carnage ahead of me. When someone falls in in front of you it's very difficult to do anything to avoid them as you suddenly have sixteen feet of mast lying across your path. They were falling like skittles, or dominoes, or anything else that tends to fall over. Perhaps being further back was an advantage, as I was able to pick my line. I decided to give them room and sail a safe path well clear of the buoy: not the shortest line by any means, but I wouldn't be wasting time picking myself up out of the water.

I was now closer to the top ten as we sped back to the finish. I suspected I might have an advantage over some of the sailors ahead of me as I knew we had yet to negotiate the one mile upwind section at the end to get back to the beach. I was sailing my course slalom board designed for just such a task: not as fast in a straight line, but much quicker upwind.

I rounded the last buoy out at sea and began the tack back upwind to the beach. I didn't put a foot wrong. It can be tricky tacking a short board in strong winds, but the sea was flat in the offshore wind and my tacks were quick and efficient. I soon made the beach, picked up board and rig, and ran for the finish line on the beach.

Out of 250 sailors, mostly men, I had finished 5th, and first woman.

The winner of the race, my team leader of the manufacturer I sailed for, was waiting on the beach to greet me. I could see on his face the delight of seeing me finish so high.

Women's windsurfing went up a notch in the estimation of the male majority that day.

That same spot on my local beach holds one further memory I'll always cherish.

I'd taken part that year in the UK leg of the Windsurfing World Cup. Unfortunately there hadn't been enough wind for legal racing, so we'd just had some fun races and put on freestyle displays for the crowds on the beach. I got an equal share of the prize fund, which was nice, but I'd have preferred the opportunity to earn some extra money by racing. It was a fun week at the beach though.

A month later, with the World Cup far from my mind, I was once again at the same spot on my local beach. I'd finished my session and was de-rigging my sail when I sensed a girl hovering nearby accompanied by her father. I heard him say:
"Go on ask her. She won't mind!".
He gently pushed her forward and a timid voice said:
"Can I have your autograph please?".
She held out the official Windsurfing World Cup programme, open at my name.

I was so flattered! I also felt a little embarrassed. It felt great though that I was somebody for a child to look up to in the world of windsurfing: a woman making it in a man's world.

It only happened one time, but yes, I gave someone my autograph.

# For Face Sake

In the abbreviated world of Twitter we often see FFS in tweets, and it confuses the hell out of me. To the world at large it's an expletive: *For Fuck's Sake*. I do wish trans women would stop using the acronym in the expletive sense. On planet trans it stands for *Facial Feminisation Surgery*.

I was never the prettiest of women, but I was undeniably female. I blended into society largely unnoticed. I say *largely* because on mercifully rare occasions I did get misgendered. Such occasions were mostly when I was at my most unkempt: for example appearing dishevelled fresh out of bed to answer the postman.

I remember pulling into a motorway services after a national series windsurfing event and parking squarely and properly in one of the few spaces available. I was dressed in shorts and sweatshirt, in a rather gender neutral style, with salt encrusted wild hair. On returning to my car I encountered an old guy who was looking rather flustered and apparently unable to get in his car despite the standard, and more than adequate, gap between our cars. As I approached my car he launched into a tirade of abuse, the argument being not about how much space I'd left him, but the fact that I'd dared to park next to him. I couldn't really argue back because yes, I had parked next to him, and I just let him vent his spleen and wait for him to calm down. He didn't calm down, and now seemed to object to my presence on planet earth. The windsurfing gear seemed to label me as some sort of drop out in his eyes. (In fact, windsurfers tend to be high wage earners due to the high cost of equipment.) My inner calm was suddenly shattered though when he addressed me as "young man". I lost it.
"If you choose to launch into a personal attack on someone, based on nothing more than how she looks, then please have the common decency to get her gender correct!"

If you are a non-trans, cisgender, person, then maybe you have had incidents when someone has misgendered you, but I suspect for most people you have not. Maybe you have shrugged off a misgendering without a second thought. For me, that simple "young man" ruined my day. I drove away from the services feeling completely deflated, totally crushed. It was as if all the pain I'd been through with transition was wasted: in the eyes of the world I was still male. My gender identity isn't just an internalised notion; it really matters to me that society sees me as female.

Many people are unaware they lead a privileged life. Most men are unaware the advantage they have in being male: they have male privilege. Equally many never experience racism: they have white privilege. A more subtle privilege most non-trans people are unaware they have is cisgender privilege. To walk into a room and have no one question your gender is a powerful thing. To walk into a women's toilet and not have someone question your right to be there is a privilege. To not have other people decide your gender, despite your protests, is a privilege. To not feel you have to reveal your medical history before sleeping with someone is a privilege. To not have someone say "what's your *real* name" when you tell them your name, is a privilege. Trans people do not have this privilege.

Misgendering a trans person hurts. It hurts a lot.

Some trans people are out and proud: they tell the world they are trans and if people aren't ok with that then that is their problem. I'm proud of being a trans woman, but very few people know I'm trans. I write under a pseudonym. I'm proud, but I'm not out. For me it hurts when people clock me as trans. It's rare it happens, but it does happen. Only once though has someone asked me to my face whether I'm trans. Correction: only once has someone assumed I'm trans and then asked me about it.

I was in my local shopping mall and there was a promotional stand for cable TV. I'd been considering signing up for some time, and decided that maybe now was the moment. I was dressed rather smartly, in a skirt, and wearing makeup; I was someone to be taken seriously. Of course, they'd have sold me cable if I'd been wearing rags, but I felt confident and in control. I discussed the options with the cable woman and elected to go for the combined TV, broadband and phone deal. She filled in the forms, writing my name and date of birth, and without saying anything she ticked the box marked *female*. She then proceeded to fill out all the other details for me. As she was completing the last fields, out of the blue she asked: "When did you transition?"

I was shocked. This had never happened to me before. I'm sure some people had assumed I was trans in the past. My best friend had once asked my boyfriend, who didn't know I was trans at the time, "Is there something *different* about Anne?". Nobody had ever asked me to my face before! She could see I was flustered.
"I'm sorry, it's me and my big mouth, I'm always doing this. I didn't mean to offend."
I answered her question, and she seemed a really nice genuine person, but once more it caused me some inner turmoil. I hadn't been misgendered, but I had been clocked, albeit in a very caring but blunt way.

What was it about me that screamed at best 'trans' and at worst 'man'?

It's very difficult to be objective about your own face. I would look in the mirror and see an unattractive woman. I could see a certain masculinity in my face, but what was it about my features that determined that? Was it my nose? I didn't have a clue. Ask me to draw a female face and a male face and apart from the hair they'd be largely the same.

With the advent of the Internet my window on the world was beginning to open. Until now I'd only ever met one other trans woman, and images of trans women were confined to the three biographies I'd read and occasional images in the media. I was now seeing images of other trans women. I was so jealous of the pretty trans women, but I was also seeing images of trans women who looked more like me. What was the difference? Was it the nose? The chin? It concerned me that the more masculine face meant an unattractive face. Why should that be? What was the difference?

Around the start of the millennium I came across the website of Professor Lynn Conway, a computer pioneer, and now trans activist. She published details of a procedure known as Facial Feminisation Surgery, FFS, which seemed to produce remarkable results in transforming a markedly masculine face into a feminine one. I looked at some of the before and after photos and was amazed. The examples were all the work of an American maxillofacial surgeon called Dr Douglas Ousterhout. At that time there was no one doing similar work in the UK. Could I dare to go all the way to America for surgery?

I started to understand the differences between a masculine face and a feminine one. The most immediate difference, and one that I'd perceived as 'drag queen face' without understanding why, was the brow ridge or boss. Under the influence of testosterone, men develop a heavy brow - a ridge of bone under the eyebrows. In some men it's very noticeable, in others less so. I didn't think this was something that I was particularly afflicted with.

The one thing I did see in my face was my nose. Maybe I should rephrase that? I'd always thought my nose was somewhat larger than you'd expect for a girl. This was borne out by the details of FFS: nearly all the procedures involved a nose job. It wasn't always just about size: the way the nose comes down from the brow can have an impact in the perceptions of male and female.

One of the main differentiators between male and female is the chin. I guess I should have already known this, having grown up with *Desperate Dan* in *The Dandy* comic, with his lantern jaw. Women generally have pointy chins, men have squarer chins. This was not a problem I thought I suffered from particularly. I really had no idea.

FFS is a palette of surgical procedures. Other treatments can include modifying the hairline, plumping the lips, bringing the cheek bones forward, and other cosmetic enhancements to complement the look, such as a face lift, and removal of bags under the eyes. I don't intend this chapter to be a surgical almanac.

I now knew what was available but still didn't really understand how this applied to my face. Try as I might I couldn't be objective about my own features. Unless I was prepared to go to America though, this was all fairly academic. I didn't know at the time, but I was playing a waiting game. I was waiting for the UK surgeon Brian Musgrove to start performing FFS.

I played my waiting game for two or three years, monitoring online forums and researching the subject. I then started to hear about a surgeon operating out of Manchester and getting good results with his FFS. This was my time. I had discovered the work of Mr Brian Musgrove, consultant maxillofacial and facial plastic surgeon.

I contacted Brian and he was happy to see me, but first I had to get a referral from my GP. I had a very good relationship with my new GP and considered her a friend, but was aware that FFS would be something new to her. I printed off the details of the procedure from Lynn Conway's website and booked an appointment with her. She was fascinated by the subject and very happy to refer me. Within a fortnight I had my appointment booked to see Brian.

And so I was off to Manchester to see the wizard, the wonderful wizard who would not be giving me a heart, a brain, or courage, but would give me that one thing a trans woman treasures above all: the unquestioned perception from society that I was female.

A quick introduction to Brian and then photos and X-rays were taken from various angles before the main consultation. Brian questioned me about my own perceptions of my features, and immediately revealed what I already knew: I had no idea. Whereas I'd thought my brow wasn't particularly prominent, Brian had other ideas. He asked me what I thought my best feature was and I thought it my jaw line; he thought differently. My nose was the one thing I was sure about, but he again pointed out something I wasn't aware of: I had a deviated septum. My left nostril was much narrower than my right, and the extra piece of cartilage I had in my left nostril wasn't extra, but should have been located centrally at the tip. If anyone questioned me about my surgery, I now had a medical reason for a nose job: to correct my deviated septum.

My menu selections had been made: I was to have brow boss reduction, nose reduction and correction of the deviated septum, my chin was to be narrowed, my jaw bone reduced, and I was to have a tracheal shave to reduce my Adam's apple. There was another procedure he recommended, to have cheek implants, but as this was too much for one session of surgery, it was left as an option for later.

What was I going to tell my work colleagues? I wasn't keen on telling them I was about to have extensive reconstruction work on my face. As luck would have it I was nearing the end of my current project. I got permission to take three weeks holiday, so no questions about sick leave, and I would return to work on a new project with new colleagues. Brian reckoned after three weeks the bruising should have gone, with only swelling remaining. There was a hopeful bonus that swelling along the jaw line would disguise the work I'd had done, and only reveal my new profile gradually.

Some weeks later I was in my surgical gown in the private hospital in Manchester. It wasn't the best start when the anaesthetist walked in and said:
"Are you the blepharoplasty[10]?"
"Er, no!"
He wasn't even my anaesthetist! Fortunately everything from that point onwards went as it should. I had my consults, signed the papers, went to theatre, counted back from ten and the next thing I knew, I had a new face.

Books on trans lives often feature graphic descriptions of surgery, and in particular the vaginoplasty. Why do people enjoy reading accounts of Genital Reconstruction Surgery? I find that a little odd. I won't be describing my lower surgery in this book, but I found the method used for the chin and jaw profiling, and particularly the method used for the brow boss reduction, incredible. If you are of sensitive disposition, I suggest you don't read the next two paragraphs.

My first description, but not necessarily the first surgical procedure, is my chin and jaw reduction. To gain access to the bone, a cut is made inside the mouth along the bottom edge of the lower gums. The lower lip can then be peeled down to expose the bone. The square end of my chin bone is sawn away on each side to reduce the width and give a more triangular look to the chin. Bone was also removed from the back of the jaw, to lighten the jawline. It's an undetectable cut with no external scar, although I did wonder if my dentist ever noticed: he never said anything.

The gruesome aspect of having your lip peeled down is nothing compared to the brow boss procedure. It can be summed up by the cut that is made: a bitemporal coronal incision. The surgeon cuts from above the ear, right over the top of the head, and down to the other ear. The whole scalp can then be rolled forward and down to expose the brow bone: an extreme face peel! Not all procedures are done this way: in a lot of cases a cut is made along the hair line. The hairline cut has the advantage of being able to bring the hairline forward, but leaves a subtle scar along the hairline, which could

---

[10] Eyelid surgery, e.g. removing bags under the eyes.

be visible if the hair is worn up. I had a full head of hair, and so the bitemporal coronal incision was used, burying the scar across the top of the head. The cut has to be made that far back to avoid cutting the nerves across the top of the head. I was warned to expect nerve damage, but no nerves were actually being cut. With the scalp and face peeled down, the brow ridge is exposed. The excess bone is removed and the area above the ridge filled in with bone cement: the cement is permanent and becomes part of the bone, never needing maintenance.

If we have the squeamish readers back, the two procedures remaining are the nose job and the tracheal shave. If you are of extremely sensitive disposition, then I'll meet you at the next paragraph. The nose job was typical of the art: the cartilage and bone were reduced, working through the nostrils. The added complication for me was the deviated septum: I'd been warned that due to the elastic nature of cartilage he might not be able to fully straighten my distorted septum, but it would be a huge improvement. He also repositioned the displaced cartilage centrally at the end of the septum. As all work was carried out through the nostrils there would be no external scars. The one externally visible scar was the tracheal shave: a small incision was made above the Adam's apple, and the prominent cartilage cut away.

The above list of procedures took a total of nine hours. To me it was over in an instant. I counted down from ten, and next I knew I was waking up on the gurney with a new face: a bruised, battered, very ugly face!

I had known what to expect from photos of other surgeries, so I wasn't actually shocked by what I saw. There was a cast on my nose, as expected, and flanking it were the two most deeply purple black eyes I've ever seen. I really looked beaten up. I hoped my cousin was going to be prepared for this when she arrived to pick me up. My chin and lips were badly swollen and I realised straight away that I was going to have to be very careful eating in the next few days with the stitches across my lower gums.

The most amazing change though was only obvious to me. The work done on my brow was quite subtle, and visually there wasn't an immediately obvious change, at least not to me looking straight on in the mirror. When I ran my fingers across my forehead though, to explore my new contours, wow! It felt incredible! My forehead felt so smooth. It was a really alien experience reaching up to touch your face, and feeling what seemed like someone else's face instead. I couldn't stop stroking my forehead. It felt so different, but it felt so good.

One of the less promising signs though, was the numbness I felt in my chin and on top of my head. Brian wasn't overly concerned by this though, as he had warned me of temporary nerve damage. As everything had gone well, he saw no reason to believe I wouldn't get full sensation back, and in fact scalp sensation returned after only a few months. The numbness in my chin took a lot longer to recede. For almost two years it felt like I didn't have full control of my lower lip: it didn't affect eating or talking, but when I grimaced I felt the numbness in one of the muscles on the left of my chin. To be fair to Brian, this is exactly what he said might happen. I'm happy to say my grimace is now as expressive as it ever was, and no lasting damage.

Back to my recovery in the hospital, I was given an on-demand intravenous morphine machine to play with: oblivion at the touch of a button. I don't recall using it though. I've had some fairly major surgeries in my time, with foot surgery and lung surgery in addition to my vaginoplasty, and I've never experienced much pain. I think I'm one of the lucky ones!

A few days later my cousin arrived to take me back to stay with my Aunt for a few weeks of recuperation. She and her husband seemed remarkably calm when they saw me, as did my Aunt when we arrived home. I guess I'd coached them well about what to expect.

One of the worst aspects to recovery was that my nose remained entirely blocked with congealed blood for almost a week after the operation. I'd been given a syringe and some vials of sterile saline to douche my nasal passages. I was so relieved when finally I was able to breath through my nose again. My nostrils now seemed to have the same size: my breathing was no longer biased towards my right nostril.

As I couldn't get to my own GP two hundred miles away, I had been told that if I wanted I could remove the nose cast myself after a week. I decided that rather than risk scaring the patients at my Aunt's village surgery, I would take the DIY approach. I found a suitably blunt dinner knife blade and very gingerly worked it up under the fibreglass cast to loosen the double sided tape that held it in place. My Aunt was rather worried about all this, but it seemed to be going ok. I eventually freed the tape and carefully lifted the cast.

Wow!

This was the most visually striking change. There was still some swelling and bruising, but there before me in the mirror was a girl's nose. As with my forehead, I immediately explored its new contours with my fingers. I held my new nose between finger and thumb. It felt so small! Just as with my forehead, my brain map of where all the parts of my body were, was being fooled. It felt so strange feeling someone else's nose. It felt so good!

The next stage of recovery was to have the staples removed from across the top of my head. Yes, staples! I'd never experienced this before: it felt like someone had fitted a zipper between my ears. It was so strange washing my hair, with baby shampoo, and having to wash carefully around these lumps of metal sticking out of my head. I believe staples are used to close large wounds because they are faster and stronger, but maybe it's also easier when working amongst the hair.

I drove back up to the hospital in Manchester for my checkup and staple removal. Brian seemed very happy with my progress and so I went off to the treatment room for the nurse to use her staple remover on me. It was summer and I was wearing a spaghetti strap top which revealed a little cleavage. The nurse was working over my shoulder and had a full view down my décolletage.
"You have lovely boobs. Do you have implants?"
"Thankyou! No they're all home grown."
That was the first time I'd ever been asked that! As a nurse in a plastic surgery clinic one would have thought she could spot implants. Assuming she knew I was trans because I was a FFS patient, then maybe she's used to trans women having breast implants? Did she think she had a licence to enquire about surgery? I really didn't mind the question, and was in fact quite flattered, but I can't help thinking she wouldn't have asked it if it wasn't for me being trans. By all means people, compliment me on my boobs; I love it. Just don't think you have free license to quiz trans people about their surgeries.

My three weeks of recovery were up and it was time to start back at work. The swelling around my jaw was still there, but concealed the profiling work to some extent. The bruising under my eyes had gone, and my face generally looked pretty good. The only issues were that I felt the scar on my neck was rather too visible, and might attract questions, and the wound hadn't fully healed across my head, with some wet blood visible through my hair. I wasn't so concerned about my scalp, as I figured my hair would hide the wound pretty well. The scar on my neck I tried to cover with concealer and powder, and reckoned I did a pretty good job of covering it.

I went several days without comment from anyone. It helped that I was on a new project and they didn't know me that well. I then went for coffee with an old friend. As we sat at the table catching up on events she suddenly said:
"Oh my god, what have you done? You're bleeding!"
My hair wasn't covering the wound as well as I'd hoped! I don't like lying but I stretched the truth a little.
"I've had a breathing problem corrected. They fixed my deviated septum - see - but they had to remove some bone around my nasal cavity, and to do that they had to go in from under my hairline"
Now that is all true apart from the fact that the nasal cavity is a lot lower than I was indicating. She seemed happy with the explanation if a little shocked. I wonder what she really thought?

Comment number two came from my best friend a week later.
"You're covering up a scar on your neck. How did you get that?"
"It's called a tracheal shave. I've had a prominent Adam's apple reduced. I've also had some of the masculine features of my face feminised. I'm trans."

So much for avoiding awkward questions!

I can't believe how casually I came out to her. There was no planning, and no rehearsal. I just said it straight out with no drama.

She took it badly. Things were awkward between us from then on. A while later I asked if she'd told her husband.
"Ooh no. I don't think he could handle it."

I think that pretty much summed up her attitude towards me. We haven't socialised since. We occasionally bump into each other at work, and she's civil to me, but that appears to be the end of that relationship.

Comment number three came from my hairdressers. The head wound had dried up, but there was still quite a large scab over the wound. I mentioned this to them as I was concerned that they shouldn't knock it when combing out my hair. It never occurred to me that the colouring I was about to have might not be advisable over a fresh wound.

I was suddenly the centre of attention, with first the senior colourist, and then the manager peering through my hair. They could see that the wound stretched over the top of my head, and inevitably they asked what I'd had done.
"I've had a lump of bone removed. I don't really want to talk about it."
That shut them up. I wonder what they thought? I just had a cut and blow dry - no colour.

I found it odd that no one ever commented about changes to my appearance. The changes were subtle, but they were there to see. It certainly helped that the swelling concealed some of the change and slowly revealed my new chin over a period of months. It also helped that I lost twenty pounds over the next year as I started to ramp up the mileage I was running. People later commented how much thinner my face looked in photos of me running. My family couldn't really describe the changes they saw, other than to say that I looked more *feminine* - well that's a relief!

Having gone from total ignorance of what makes a face masculine or feminine, I am now far more aware of differences, making me even better at the game we trans people like to play called "Spot the trans person". The main difference when we play it, as opposed to when transphobes play it, is that a spot might result in a subtle nod, or gentle smile, rather than finger pointing and sniggering. My appreciation of facial differences was also brought into play in the most unusual of settings, when I watched the movie *The Incredibles.* It's a Pixar movie about a family of superheroes. Like most 3D rendered animations, it portrays humans in cartoon form. Features get exaggerated in the cartooning process so that the small pointy female chin becomes smaller and pointier, and the large square male chin becomes a lantern jaw. The brow, the nose, the chin: suddenly I could see how the artists had drawn the characters to be immediately identifiable as male or female. Why did it take thousands of pounds worth of surgery for me to see that?

Clearly, being able to analyse cartoon drawings is a major benefit of facial surgery. I think the biggest benefit though is this: since the surgery I haven't had a single misgendering. I've appeared at the door with unkempt bird's nest hair, dressing gown, no makeup, and been addressed as "love", "dear", "madam". Isn't that what any trans woman ever wants?
The surgery may be expensive, but what price confidence and happiness? It was very much worth it!

I wonder whether to have the second stage of surgery that Brian Musgrove suggested: cheek implants. There is much to be said for having an implant free body. I'm still undecided.

# I am a woman

One of my sources of information prior to transition was Caroline Cossey's book *I am a Woman*. Caroline modelled under the name Tula, of Bond girl and Smirnoff vodka advert fame, and was outed by the press. After the uproar of her 'deception', her name was removed from the credits of *For Your Eyes Only*. Her book came out in 1982 in my second year at university, just at the time when I was starting to explore my gender identity and expression. I bought it as soon as it was released. I read it twice. Her story was mine.

In the pre-Internet years, information was hard to come by. My early years were informed almost entirely by tabloid news stories. They were sensational stories, holding up trans women, never trans men, to be ridiculed. These were not positive stories. These people were portrayed as grotesques, freaks. I was grotesque, a freak.

When Tula was outed, the headlines were all variations on a theme of a top model was really a man: she had spent years deceiving the public. Despite the title of her book 'I am a Woman', a title with a message if ever there was one, I somehow bought into the tabloid message that Tula and I were not women. It would take me years to shake that conditioning.

It was hard to find positive stories back then. From a young age I was scouring the local libraries looking for information about my sisters. The first book I found was Jan Morris *Conundrum*. I couldn't borrow the book from the library as Mum would find it and I felt it would most likely out me. I was so paranoid back then. Any feminine behaviour I displayed had been swiftly dealt with and I'd been left deeply ashamed and frightened of giving any clues to me being trans. I visited the library each day and read Conundrum in the library. That was the book that told me I could be who I wanted to be. I was a little concerned that I might have to go to Casablanca for surgery, but for the first time I saw my path lighting up in front of me.

Another book I read in the library was Gore Vidal's satirical novel *Myra Breckinridge*. I also read its sequel *Myron*. This was hardly a source of information, being a pornographic attack on puritanical America, but the eponymous heroine was a trans woman and it was an enjoyable read. My abiding memory of the book was how Gore Vidal had replaced all the rude words with names of American establishment figures responsible for censorship. Myra would refer to her breasts as her 'glorious Father Hills'. I was clearly impressionable if I can remember that nearly forty years later! It's a shame it's another example of works of fiction sexualising trans women.

At university I had access to the university library which gave more scope for self exploration. It didn't really help. The learned papers and writings of Harry Benjamin just seemed to imply I was at best a homosexual in need of validation, or at worst a fetishist with a need to turn my body into a source of erotic fascination. To further injure my self esteem, I put in a request to retrieve a book called *The Other Women* from the stores. It was a collection of photographs of drag queens on the Berlin gay scene. I'll never forget the withering look I got from the woman at the desk when she handed it over. I don't know what she imagined were my motivations, but she clearly didn't have a very high opinion of me. I might as well have been in drag myself when collecting the book. Yet again I was made to feel ashamed of who I was.

Another book to come out in 1982 was *April Ashley's Odyssey*. I bought the hard back edition as soon as it was published - no waiting for the paperback for this impoverished student. That book was significant for two things, both centring on April's divorce case. Firstly it told me that I would never be a woman, able to marry a man, in the eyes of the law. April's divorce case was the first of its kind, where it was less about divorce and more about proving April wasn't legally female. It remained legal precedent until the Gender Recognition Act came into effect in 2005. Secondly, and my heart goes out to April, having this dragged through the courts, it would seem that to be able to consummate a marriage, you must be able to insert four fingers into the vagina. That odd fact stayed with me for years to come and would prove to be my downfall. I will return to that later in this book.

The book that resonated most with me was Caroline Cossey's book *I am a Woman*. She was telling my story, ignoring for a moment the stunningly beautiful looks and the amazing modelling career. At least she was a near contemporary who didn't have to go to Casablanca for her surgery. There was a curious aspect of the book though that didn't sit well with me: the title.

Tula/Caroline is a woman. She is a stunningly beautiful woman. I am a woman. I just couldn't convince myself of that. My whole life I'd had society, be it my parents or the tabloid press, telling me I was a freak: *look at the weird boy who likes to wear dresses*. My self esteem was at rock bottom. I knew what I had to do, but I couldn't break away from the feelings indoctrinated into me that I was something other than female, regardless of how I felt inside.

After transition I was socialised completely as female. I was referred to as 'she'. My mail was addressed to Miss... My medical records stated female. Eventually I would even have a birth certificate with 'girl' on it. Yet if someone were to ask me if I was a man or a woman, ignoring for the moment the embarrassment of someone not knowing my gender, I would flush as I replied "I am a woman". I would fail a lie detector test.

Shortly after my surgery, a little over a year after transition, I took my first trip abroad presenting as female. For the trip I was wearing skin tight jeans, a bright yellow bat wing top, and a little makeup. It's again curious to note that my emotionally charged memories are burned in with the exact details of what I was wearing. I felt relaxed. I'd been correctly gendered and addressed by all the staff, and from the lack of reaction of the passengers I hadn't been clocked by anyone. I took my seat and the little girl in front was standing in her seat looking back at me. She smiled, I smiled, and with total innocence she suddenly asked:
"Are you a boy or a girl?"
Clearly I should have calmly replied to tell her I was a girl, but it knocked me for six. I was flustered. Why couldn't I answer her? Her mother saved me the trouble though:
"Don't be so rude to the lady!"
Why couldn't I answer? Was I not convinced of the answer?

It left me with a lot of questions of what the child saw that her mother didn't.

There seems to be an intellectual process at work, where we are able to rationalise the gender signals coming from others and consciously ignore any contradictory signals that are in the minority. In the young though, this process is absent, and just one indicator such as a square chin or brow boss comes shining through like a beacon and screams male. I hadn't had Facial Feminisation Surgery back then - the surgical procedures weren't yet available as a FFS package. I didn't have a particularly masculine face, but some of the markers, such as chin, brow and nose were definitely there.

This intellectual override process was again demonstrated in the tragic case of my friend's husband. He was a lovely man, and I felt completely at ease with him. There was never any indication that he viewed me as anything other than completely female. He knew me before and after my FFS, and like everyone else, did not seem to notice any change in my appearance, despite the, to me, very obvious softening of my features.

Then he was diagnosed with Alzheimer's Disease.

His slip into dementia was swift and tragic. My friend had to face up to the fact that the man she had married had gone. It was heartbreaking to see. There were symptoms such as violent behaviour which made him impossible to live with, but the real tragedy was that the man my friend loved just wasn't in there any more. He didn't know who anybody was. He would often just talk gibberish, latching on to strange tangential thoughts and muttering them over and over.

He made me feel very uncomfortable. He had the same reaction every time he met me. He would mutter under his breath:
"Nancy boy."
Nobody else seemed to notice, or tried not to say anything, but to me it was very obvious. Without his intellectual processes at work, something was flagging me up to him as male, albeit a very effeminate male. It is possible that he'd always suspected I was trans, particularly as he knew me before my FFS, and it was that memory that was surfacing. That seemed unlikely though when he didn't know who anybody else was. It seemed to me that there was some masculine vibe I was still giving off, despite a whole load of feminine ones, that flagged me as a 'nancy boy'.

Fearful of what others might think, I never tried to correct him.

For years I couldn't look someone in the face and say "I am a woman" without feeling awkward. When talking about my childhood to someone who didn't know my past, which was just about everyone, I couldn't say "When I was a little girl".

There is a symptom of my early imprinting which surprises me to this day: sensitivity to my old dead name. I'm fully sensitised though to my real, i.e. female, name. If someone says my name quietly at the other end of the office I immediately know they are talking about me. If someone calls my real name, it immediately breaks me out of whatever I'm doing as I turn to look in their direction. However, if someone calls my dead, i.e. male, name, although I don't consciously react and turn round, I can still feel an emotional response. It feels like a slightly prickly sensation. It may not be obvious to anyone, but I'm fairly sure it would show on a lie detector. I have never told anyone my old name. I never will. It's dead. It's irrelevant. It worries me though that someone adept at cold reading, a mentalist to use the American sense of the word, would be able to determine my dead name with just a few simple techniques. Am I being unnecessarily paranoid?

It's only in recent years, after much introspection, that I've come to realise that all the childhood behaviour that I was made to feel ashamed of, e.g. playing with dolls, wearing Mum's lipstick and heels, was actually perfectly normal behaviour for a little girl. My self image in all my earliest memories is that of a little girl. When I picture myself cowering under the dressing table, trying to get away from my father, I'm wearing a pretty dress. (To be fair, it is possible I was wearing one of Mum's dresses, but in my memory it's a girls' dress and fits me.) I can now comfortably drop into a conversation about childhood the line
"When I was a little girl..."

Equally, but again only in the last few years, I can at last be wired to a lie detector, look someone in the face, and proudly proclaim
"I am a Woman".

# Legally me

Trans people are often portrayed as deceivers: the line used by the press when reporting on crimes involving trans women is usually what I call the "Oh my god she's a man!" paradigm. I hope you are getting the message that gender identity is hard-wired and understand the fallacy behind such reporting. If any deception is being perpetrated, then it's by a pre-transition trans person, as their outer appearance is not portraying their true gender.

There was a time in the UK though when we were legally deceivers. Despite all outer appearances, my legal documentation didn't back up the fact that I was female. After transition I was able to get my National Insurance details changed, my driving licence was re-issued in my new, legal, name, but my birth certificate still stated my old name and alleged gender. My passport was ambiguous: the gender marker on old style British passports was *Mr/Miss/Mrs* in front of the name handwritten on the front - my passport had no title, as I wasn't allowed *Miss*, and so for someone who knew what to look for I was outed the moment I showed my passport. Note the sexism too in requiring women to declare their marital status on the passport - *Ms* was not an option.

After my treatment by the Ministry of Defence I vowed that never again would anyone know my trans history and so when I moved jobs I did so without disclosing.

On joining the company I was sent for a full medical; again I did not disclose. I feared the consequences of declaring I was trans: I had no legal protection and as I was on six month's probation, I feared giving them a reason to dismiss me. At the medical I had the usual questions about my menstrual health, but they seemed to accept the fact that I was amenorrheic and didn't pursue the line of questioning. I failed to mention I was on HRT.

My new company had a generous remuneration package, with, for the first time in my life, private health insurance. I didn't have to answer any probing questions for the health insurance, perhaps that was the purpose of the medical, and so I didn't see any problems with not telling them I was trans. I saw no issue with this it the time, but I had no one else in my life with whom to debate the matter: I had not re-established contact with my

Aunt at that time, and so no one I had any contact with knew I was trans. It was only several years later with the birth of the Internet that I was able to get the opinion of others that I might actually be invalidating my health insurance by not telling them my trans history. I was told of claims that had been withheld on discovery of a person's trans status. I was apparently walking on thin ice!

Despite the feeling that I would at some point hit trouble over my non-disclosure stance, I never had any problems. The few times when I needed the health insurance, for a series of collapsed lung incidents followed by corrective surgery, the claims went through without issue; this was despite being horribly misgendered by the chest consultant!

I felt like an equal member of society, if a little insecure in my position of equality, except for one important aspect: I couldn't marry the man I loved. My name may have been changed on all my important documents, and on some of them the gender marker too, but when it really came down to it the law still regarded me as male. Whenever I came upon some legal registration process, be that for a change of GP, or for a television license, I always feared having to show my birth certificate: it was in my old name and quite clearly declared me as '*boy*'.

Such was the depth of my non-disclosure, it took me three years into my relationship with Dougie, before I told him I was trans. During that time I would have gladly said yes to a marriage proposal, but I would have had to say no due to my legal position. It cut me up inside to be caught like that. I wanted so much to be the same as any other woman yet I was constantly reminded I wasn't.

It had taken the law some time to catch up with trans people. When April Ashley had married the aristocrat Arthur Corbett in 1963, there seemed no reason to object to the marriage as April was clearly female. However, when things turned sour in 1970, the divorce ended up in the courts where the lawyers attempted to prove that the marriage was void from the outset on the grounds that April was, and always would be, male. Unfortunately the lawyers succeeded, and *Corbett vs Corbett* became the legal precedent which defined April, me, and all other trans people as the gender that had been entered on their birth certificates. April was such a role model for me when I was growing up, but I couldn't help a certain bitterness towards the legacy her divorce had left for me regarding the legal status of my gender.

By the turn of the century I was starting to hear stories about challenges in the European Court of Human Rights. There had been previous unsuccessful challenges, most notably by Caroline Cossey, and I didn't hold out much hope for change. It's interesting to look back now and realise how resigned I was to the fact that I was indeed a second class citizen. I had been ground down over the years by the attitudes of my parents and brother and I had very little pride in who I was. These days I would be fighting for my rights alongside others, but back then I was ashamed and in hiding, believing what my parents and society said about trans people.

In 2002 came the news that in the case *Christine Goodwin v The United Kingdom,* the European Court of Human Rights had found in favour of Christine, and recognised her as legally female and having the right to marry a man. The UK government was now obliged to change the law and consign *Corbett vs Corbett* to history. In 2005 the *Gender Recognition Act 2004* came into law and I was now given full status as female and full legal protection to go with that[11].

The law permitted a new birth certificate to be issued, stating that I'm female, or rather *'girl'* as it appears on the certificate. My dreams had been answered. I wasted no time in applying for the Gender Recognition Certificate (GRC) needed in order to get my birth certificate changed.

There was a fast-path process put in place to deal with the thousands of people who had transitioned more than six years previously, myself included, who might have problems obtaining the proof required under the rules for new transitioners. My psychiatrist had retired and my surgeon had

---

[11] In fact we don't get full protection: the law makers always seem to drop an extra clause or two in to emphasise we aren't quite first class citizens. In this case it's the right of Anglican clergy to refuse to marry trans people, apparently on 'conscientious' grounds, and also for sports organisations to exclude trans people, despite the International Olympic Committee allowing trans people to compete equally.

been struck off, so obtaining statements from them could be tricky. Fortunately I just had to swear a statement in front of a barrister that I met the requirements, and with an appropriately signed and stamped document a GRC would be mine.

The guidance was that a quick visit to my local magistrates court would be all that was required. I booked a day off work, got dressed up as if going to work, and along I went. The nerves kicked in as soon as I entered the building: I was up against officialdom, and I was going to have to out myself to various strangers. I never quite know how such encounters are going to turn out. The building was heaving with people; I guess I expected somewhere a little more hushed and dignified than somewhere more resembling a market. I fought my way to the front desk and explained that I needed a member of the bar to witness a statement for an application for a Gender Recognition Certificate. I'm not sure if they understood I was outing myself to them, but it was the fact that I was asking for the services of a lawyer in a court that seemed to cause them concern. I was told to go wait in the corridor whilst they tried to find someone.

I'm not sure how magistrates courts work, but my small request seemed to be causing an awful lot of work. Various puzzled people appeared at regular intervals, there was shaking of heads, then pointing at me, then nodding of heads, more shaking of heads, followed by hasty steps away down the corridor.

After what seemed an eternity, someone wearing the loudest pin-stripe suit I've ever seen approached me. He had a very strong air of *lawyer* about him; he wasn't wearing a legal gown, but I knew he was the guy they had been searching for the moment I saw him. For those of you who've watched UK antiques programmes and who know the antiques expert David Dickinson, then imagine him turned up a few notches. My lawyer was strikingly similar in appearance to David 'The Duke' Dickinson but with a deeper tan, louder suit, and bigger personality, as improbable as that seems.

The lawyer suggested we found a quiet room to discuss what was required. I expected a small side office, but was led to an empty court room. This was turning out to be a much grander experience than I'd imagined! I explained my circumstances and the need for a legal document to present my case to the Gender Recognition Panel. To my relief he understood what was required and sent his secretary away to prepare a suitable statement. After another hour or so, I left the court with the document that I needed.

A few weeks later I had my new birth certificate. It stated my full legal, female, name, and next to that, most importantly of all, had the word ***girl***. At long last I was legally the gender I'd been presenting to the world for more than half my life.

The re-issue of birth certificates causes raised eyebrows with some people, but understanding the validity of the new certificate is crucial to understanding the nature of being trans. My cousin had quite a problem accepting my new birth certificate. He had mapped our huge family tree, basing it on the birth and death records of the family going back several hundred years. I sent him my birth certificate, but he was very reluctant to change my name and gender on the family tree. Despite the full legal weight of my new certificate, he didn't see it as a valid historical document. I think a lot of people have difficulty with the idea of a change of birth certificate, due to the idea of it documenting a historical event. They see it as rewriting history. History is not being changed though; the document is merely being updated to correct the mistake made at the time. I was female at birth; to be fair to the doctors it would have been almost impossible to determine that at the time of birth and so *'boy'* was entered on the certificate. It is only later in life that the mistake is realised and so a correction is made to the paperwork. Nothing about me has changed, other than my external appearance and how I fit into society. The birth certificate is the mere confirmation of a gender identity I have always had.

The law is so important in the acceptance of trans people. The Equality Act of 2010 made it illegal to discriminate against trans people in areas such as housing, services, healthcare and employment. I've never needed to call upon the Equality Act. I've never needed to show my birth certificate in an official capacity and very few people have even seen it. The fact that there are legal protections there if needed though, gives me the confidence to be who I am and not be forced to hide. More crucially it sends a message about the legitimacy of transgender identities and helps create acceptance in everyday society. There is still terrible prejudice against trans people, and often the law cannot help when it comes to everyday struggles for acceptance. However, the fact that we now have equality for trans people written into law means that half the battle is won: the law leads and society follows.

I may encounter prejudice in future. I hope I never have to seek assistance from the law to enforce my rights, but I no longer have to hide who I am. Finally, I am legally, me.

# What's your real name?

I write under a pen-name. My real name is the one on my re-issued birth certificate. It is legally recognised. It is real. I chose it.

Why do people have a problem with that?

The musician *Example* is quite happy to be addressed as Elliot, that being his name - the name Example comes from his initials E.G.. *Plan B* seems amenable to being called Ben, and is credited in his drama roles under the name Ben. Address Sir Elton John as Reg, however, and you are likely to get a slap.

We seem to have a fascination with *real* names. Pub quizzes abound with answers such as Marion Morrison, Maurice Micklewhite and Norma Jeane Mortenson[12]. These stars of Hollywood delivered their performances behind a stage name. Their true identity is more closely allied with their birth name than the persona they project under the guise of their public name. As such, maybe it is valid to enquire of their birth name, in pursuit of a clue to their real persona.

I had been dating Dougie for three years before telling him I was trans, such was my fear of the consequences. Of all the things he could have said to support me, and show sympathy for my emotional state, having just opened my heart to him, the first thing he chose to say after I came out to him was: "What's your real name?"

That question crushed me. In four words he'd revealed his complete lack of understanding of me. To him I was suddenly just a façade: a performance under my stage name. The woman he loved had evaporated to be replaced by a character played by someone else: someone else with a *real name*.

---

[12] John Wayne, Michael Caine and Marilyn Monroe

I've heard trans people say "I don't mind people knowing my old name, it holds no power over me". That's great, and power to them, however I'm Rumpelstiltskin in the Grimm's fairy tales; I'm Mister Mxyztplk from the Superman comics. My old name holds great power over me: it shouldn't, but it does.

I coach athletics. In order to be able to coach children I need a Criminal Records Bureau (CRB) check. It's easy to obtain: you just fill in a form, include all your details, including all your former names, get it counter signed, and send it off. Despite having a birth certificate in my correct name, and having my gender fully recognised legally, on the face of it I was going to have to out myself to my fellow coaches and UK Athletics in order to get my CRB check. I realised this wasn't within the spirit of the law regarding gender recognition, so I did some Internet research and found a telephone number for a government department set up to deal with the unique situation we trans people find ourselves in regarding background checks. Somewhat relieved, I phoned the number and spoke to a very understanding woman who assured me she'd had the correct training to deal with me. Why do I keep hearing people tell me that they've been trained to deal with me? The Relate relationship counselling people said the same thing! Perhaps I ought to carry a card "I'm trans. Have you had the appropriate training?". Further reassured, I explained the situation, and gave her all my details including my full name.

She then demanded my old name.

Well at least she didn't ask for my *real name*!

I was taken aback! After the Gender Recognition Act and the legalisation of my gender and name, I never expected to have to ever give my old name to anyone again. I was shocked! In fact I was so shocked I was shaking.
"What if I refuse to give you my old name?"
"I'm sorry my love, but without your old name we can't run the checks and can't issue a certificate."
She was very sympathetic, but was quite firm. I'd always assumed that there must be some cross-linking or changing of old records during the Gender Recognition process, but I think gender change and name change are separate processes. I was now in tears. She clearly knew how difficult this

was for me, but couldn't budge: no name, no certificate. Finally through the sobbing, I spelt out my old name for her. I was a wreck.

Why does my old name hold such power over me? In saying my old name I'm not at that instant outing myself, as whoever is asking for the name surely knows I'm trans already. It's the ungendering effect of revealing it. It's the male identity that comes with the name. In its revealing, my gender seems to be taken from me, and the proud confident woman becomes the scared confused boy of my childhood. That might be a subject for some therapy!

It's not just the abstract notion of male gender evoked by the name: the name brings back memories of my former self. I really don't like looking at photos of the old me. In fact I got rid of most of those old photos: only my graduation photo remains, and I've often considered burning it. It's not just me that purged myself of the old images: my mother and father, who I'd assumed would want to hang onto images of the male me and pretend female me didn't exist, also got rid of all my old photos. They effectively wiped any memory of me from their lives. The one saving grace, was that my mum hung onto my graduation photo, unbeknownst to my dad. That is the reason I still have it. I think my mum still had some love for me, but wasn't allowed to show it because of my overbearing father. In a sense, my graduation photo is one of the last remaining links to my mother.

I recently got back in touch with Mike, the drummer from my student band. He knew I'm trans, as I'd come out to him at university, but he had never had the pleasure of meeting the real me. Having contacted him on Facebook, I didn't want to have to tell him my old name, so there then followed a guessing game where I had to describe who I was. Despite his terrible memory he soon realised who I was and my old name was safe. He then came out with a frankly brilliant alternative for *old name/dead name/former name:* he calls it my *maiden name.* It seems so appropriate; I just love it. It might get confusing if I get married though.
"What's your maiden name Mrs Cognito?"
"Henry Smith."[13]

---

[13] I'm sure I don't need to spell it out, but here it is anyway: ***that is not my***

So you want to know my real name?

Go to hell!

---

***old name!***

# The fear

*November 2012*

I've been dating a guy for a few weeks now. Last night we had a romantic meal: just the two of us, fine food, wine, candles, soft music. Afterwards there was holding of hands, there was cuddling, there was snogging. He told me that after our previous date, when we kissed goodbye, he felt sparks. He's a lovely guy, kind and considerate, and we seem very compatible. Today I should be walking on cloud nine; I should be full of the joys of new romance. Instead I feel down. I have a sense of foreboding. There are dark clouds on the horizon. Will the relationship last beyond the end of the month?

He doesn't know I'm trans.

It's at times like these that I feel like shaking my fists at the sky and screaming:
"Yes I'm trans, but I deserve to be loved like anyone else. I have the same feelings as any other woman. Why should my medical history be relevant to this relationship?"

Sadly, as I've proved time and again, men seem to think my medical history is extremely relevant to a relationship.

I'm partly to blame in the failure of my relationships. Whenever the issue of disclosure comes up I'm on the defensive. I never approach the task of disclosure with any positivity; if I see it as a problem then why should my boyfriend think any different? Do I still see myself as male? Well no, but my fear is that he might. Do I see myself as having a problem? I think I do, and I believe the media are at fault.

All my life I've been bombarded with negative images of trans people. We are portrayed as sexual aggressors, as sexual deviants; it's all about *sex*. There's a very good reason why trans people, myself included, no longer use the word *transsexual*, but prefer simply *trans*: the word *sexual* brings with it way too much baggage.

For years we've been over-sexualised in the media: we are portrayed as either objects of sexual fascination and fetishistic desire, or as creatures whose own fetishistic desires make us objects of ridicule. Who in their right mind would be attracted to someone ridiculous and pathetic? The need for a man to express a female gender identity is seen as motivated by sexual desire. The books use terms such as *autogynephilia* - being sexually aroused by seeing oneself as having a female body - and *transvestic fetishism,* both listed as *paraphilia* i.e. sexual arousal not part of *normal* sexual behaviour. There is still an attitude that any form of sexual behaviour that isn't vanilla sex between a man and a woman is not *normal*. Remember that when these terms were first used to describe trans people, homosexuality was still listed as a mental disorder. Note too, that while *autogynephilia* has largely been discredited, *transvestic fetishism* is still listed in the Diagnostic and Statistical Manual of Mental Disorders (DSM-5) as exactly that: a mental disorder.

In my formative years I identified with the media images of trans people. In dramas I immediately felt sympathy for the trans person, put there for the rest of the world to laugh at or vilify. While Forest Whittaker's character was throwing up in *The Crying Game,* following the big reveal, I felt sorry for Jaye Davidson's trans character Dil trying to find love in a hostile world.

The situation for Jaye Davidson's character is particularly difficult, as of course the presence of a penis immediately signals *man* in most people's eyes, and I have some sympathy for that reaction. There are however many reasons why a trans woman may not want or cannot have surgery, and it takes a special kind of guy to see beyond that; those guys exist but are very difficult to find.

The revelation of the penis in *The Crying Game* is of course there for the shock value: *"Oh my god, she's a man!"*. The revelation that a character is trans is always just that: a revelation. Despite trying to act like it's not, I always go into the process of disclosure with some sort of belief that this is a moment of revelation. I confess that I have had fun with disclosure on a couple of occasions, doing the big reveal, but I had less to lose on those occasions. The one time I just casually happened to mention I was trans to my best friend, almost without thinking about it, after she asked about the tracheal shave scar, it came as such a shock to her she's hardly spoken to me since.

Just what is it that I'm revealing? How do I change in people's eyes that I can no longer be a lover or a friend?

These people have been bombarded with the same images as I have. They've been indoctrinated with false notions of trans women as sexual predators. The sad fact is that what changes in people's eyes at the moment of disclosure is that I cease to be female: like Dil in *The Crying Game,* I'm revealed to be a man.

There was a recent newspaper story of a Belgian man who discovered his wife of nineteen years was trans. The British press ran with "used to be a man", "born a man", and quoted the guy as saying "I feel I've been assaulted" and "My world collapsed". His lawyer was quoted as saying "That person has deliberately deceived him for years, even scammed". The Nigerian Tribune had the headline: "Height of deception: Husband discovers wife is a man after 19 years". It's clear from the story that the marriage had already broken down before the disclosure, and we see a bitter man prepared to take his poor wife, whom he loved for nineteen years, through the courts and destroy her. The press though side with the husband and portray the wife as the deceiver.

The image of trans people as deceivers is something we see time and again in the press. What hope do we have of gently disclosing that we are trans against that background? In the eyes of, I'd dare say most, people we cease to be women from the moment of disclosure and transform into men. There is a word for this process: ungendering.

Where once the fact that I'm 5'10" was of no consequence other than to put me at the upper end of the female height spectrum (in fact, of the three women working in my part of the office, I'm average height), my height is now a consequence of my male chromosomes[14]. My size nine feet, although

---

[14] How many people actually know if they are XX or XY? Intersex conditions are more common than you might imagine. I've never been tested.

average for my height, are now man-feet. My elegant hands with long fingers, perfect for a pianist, are now 'a dead giveaway'.

Not everyone finds these slightly male features unattractive in a woman though. In fact there are men out there who have a preference for trans women. I must admit, I once told a friend that I wouldn't date a man who wanted to date me because I was trans. I am slowly revising that opinion though. The expression *tranny chaser* is used rather derogatorily to describe a certain type of guy attracted to trans women. Many of these guys come across as a bit creepy, seemingly entirely motivated by sex. Guys, when you meet a trans woman, it's not a good idea to make your opening line a question about what surgery she's had. I once spent an afternoon with a guy, dating me because I was trans, and it was the most boring afternoon of my life: when a guy's main interest in life is trans women, it doesn't make for great conversation with a trans woman.

Why do we need to label people according to their preference for certain types of women? Just as we have *tranny chaser* we also have *chubby chaser*. There is an attitude that if a guy is attracted to anyone outside the norms of feminine beauty then he's not right, and needs a label. We all have particular preferences, be they redheads, blondes, tall women, voluptuous women, athletic women, or trans women. Who are we to judge what is normal? If a man finds me attractive then he is just demonstrating good taste.

There is also the spectre of sexuality hanging over a man's attraction to trans women. If a guy has a preference for pre-op or non-op trans women, then the assumption is he's gay, with the social stigma still attached to that. Gay men are not attracted to trans women: gay men prefer men, and excuse me for pointing that out. I don't believe that attraction to trans women is an entirely heterosexual attraction, but if we don't get hung up on labels then frankly, who cares?

Sexuality is very much a spectrum, but we get preoccupied with placing people at fixed points on the spectrum. My personal view is that if we could do away with the idea that straight is normal, gay is not, then we'd see that people generally are far more capable of loving either sex than they currently care to admit. I base this view on the fact that many of my trans women friends get married and raise families prior to transition, and yet find they are attracted to men after transition. The wives of pre-transition trans women often express the opinion that "I can't possibly love you after transition - I'm not a lesbian", and yet some relationships survive transition and effectively become lesbian relationships. I've seen enough evidence that "I'm straight, end of story" is an over simplification.

For the first thirty years of my life I had the conviction that I was straight, and only dated men. Prior to transition I had no interest sexually in women, and never dated a woman. Post transition, I had a few brief relationships with men, followed by the one big love-of-my-life relationship with Dougie. My relationship with Dougie sadly didn't last; I was heart-broken, but I was once more a single party-girl. As my best friend and I were getting party-ready one day, she got undressed in front of me. Oh my! I couldn't keep my eyes off her! I'd never felt like this in my life before, and it worried me: I'd been so concerned about fitting into society's expectations of me as a woman, it seemed like my world had come crashing down. Was I a lesbian? One crush hardly makes me a lesbian, but I clearly wasn't as heterosexual as I'd like to think.

More recently I've come to a further realisation about my sexuality: I'm attracted to trans women. There is such honesty in a relationship between two trans women; the mutual respect and shared experience creates a very strong bond. I'm slowly coming to the realisation that my perfect partner may in fact be female.

As for my current relationship, we've got to the point in our relationship where I feel duty bound to disclose I'm trans. I have a certain amount of emotional investment in the relationship, I want the relationship to last, and I want it to move forward based on openness and honesty. I've decided I have to disclose, and it scares me.

Yet again, I'm experiencing 'The Fear'.

# The party

*September 2000*

I had been working at a customer site for a few months. Our IT people worked alongside the customer's IT people; they seemed a nice enough bunch but I didn't have much contact with them on a day to day basis. One day a guy I vaguely knew came up to me at the laser printer and said:
"Do you know Russell Reid?"
"No."
"Ah well, never mind."
The whole tone of the brief conversation struck me as odd, but I thought nothing more of it.

That weekend I was in the local computer shop, when the same guy tapped me on the shoulder.
"Sorry about the other day."
"What?"
"When I talked about Russell Reid."
"That's ok."
I had absolutely no idea what the guy was talking about. It all seemed rather strange.

A week later, again at the laser printer, almost as if I was being targeted:
"I'm coming down your way after work this evening."
How did the guy know where I lived? Was he stalking me? He continued:
"To the beauty salon on the seafront. I'm having electrolysis to remove my beard."
Oh my god! The penny dropped. He, or rather she, was trans: it was the only possible explanation. I had been targeted because she knew I was trans too.

This came as a bit of a shock; I'd been clocked by someone I worked with. I was supposedly living in stealth, with no one knowing I was trans. That dented my confidence somewhat. I guess we trans women have special skills when it comes to spotting other trans women, but even so, I felt defeated.

The reason our initial encounters had been so awkward was that I was missing one vital piece of information: Russell Reid was head of the Gender Identity Clinic at Charing Cross Hospital. She hadn't realised I'd transitioned so long ago that Russell Reid had only just started working at Charing Cross when I was there, and I was under the care of a different doctor. To be fair, she'd chosen a very discrete way of introducing herself. If only it had worked!

She was only the second trans person I'd ever met, and the first in fifteen years, such was my isolation from the trans community.

One morning soon afterwards, we were all ushered in to the main conference room for a big announcement. What followed was one of the most uncomfortable meetings I've ever had the misfortune to attend. It was her transition announcement. It was handled extremely well by the HR people, without her being present. They explained, amidst some rather childish sniggering, that she was going to be returning to work on Monday in a female role. They explained how gender identity worked as regards a female brain in a male body. They explained the need for respect and the correct use of female pronouns. She would be using the female toilets: there were a few raised eyebrows at that one. They announced her new name: Anne[15].

*That's my name! How dare she!*

I had to grit my teeth and hope nobody could see how flushed I was as I had to endure all the transphobic mutterings in the room.
"Jesus, why would anyone want to go through all that?"
"Well at least *we* don't have to share the loo with him."
"He's going to make one bloody ugly woman."

---

[15] Again, the disclaimers that Anne is my pen name, but she really did have the same name as me.

Was this the sort of crap that was spouted behind my back when I transitioned? Thank god I can live in stealth and not have to face this sort of abuse.

In the next few weeks I had to witness her go through a very difficult transition at the hands of my trans-misogynist colleagues. I felt so sorry for her, but didn't feel I could do anything without outing myself.

I had less sympathy though over the matter of football. She had been a passionate player of the game and had taken part in all the lunchtime five-a-side matches. After transition she wanted to keep playing, but the guys wouldn't let her. While I sympathised with her situation and felt they were being really horrible to her, I also felt that she should have accepted the situation and moved on. They argued that it was a men's five-a-side league and as she was a woman she wasn't allowed to play. I knew that, as there was no women's league, if any other woman had wanted to join in, they would have let her; in fact they did just that a few years later when one of the other women wanted a game. It was an argument Anne just wasn't going to win. I felt she wanted it both ways, which from a feminist stand point is great, but if you've just transitioned you're not going to win any hearts and minds by stating you are a woman but insisting on playing on a man's team. That might seem harsh but we can't have everything our way when our daily lives are a struggle simply to be recognised for who we are.

One day she invited me to a party, and explained she'd invited some of her trans friends. I accepted. I thought it would be good to meet others like me after such a long time in the wilderness.

It took a long time to get over the guilt and self-questioning that that innocent house party gave me.

When I'd first walked in to the London support group all those years ago, it had been a revelation; my initial impression had been of a place I belonged, where everyone was like me. This was different; I immediately felt ill at ease.

The party was a roughly fifty:fifty mix of trans and cisgender people. Anne's friends were naturally similar to her: the trans people at the party were all trans women, either in the early stages of transition or newly transitioned. They were mostly older than me, transitioning late in life. Her cisgender friends were more of a mix of ages, with perhaps more women than men, and a number of women roughly my age.

My attire was one source of concern. I'd dressed up in a party dress: I was wearing an electric blue crushed velvet bodycon mini dress, showing lots of leg and a fair amount of cleavage. I did look rather fab, and really stood out. I'd made an effort! Sadly, apart from one other cis woman, I seemed to be the only one to have made such an effort. Most of the cis people were in jeans. The trans women were a pretty drab bunch in very subdued colours, frumpy dresses, and generally rather unfashionable. I felt all eyes were on me, which I could have revelled in, in another situation, but here it felt like I was drawing unnecessary attention.

Another cause for concern was that it seemed I was outing myself by turning up at a party for trans people with so many cis people present. It felt like I had a big 'trans' label pinned to me. Fortunately I didn't recognise any of the cis people so it would appear that Anne hadn't invited any colleagues. Hopefully I wouldn't have to deal with any rumours at work of me being trans. I'd witnessed some horrible transphobia in the previous weeks, and suddenly felt that my workplace wasn't quite so welcoming as I'd previously felt.

My main cause for concern, was my own reaction to the appearance of the trans women. My experience of trans women so far had been of people like Caroline Cossey and April Ashley in books, my mentor Judy, and of course myself. The trans women at the party were rather different. My first impression, and I hate myself for saying this, was that they looked like men in dresses. It was obvious that many were wearing wigs, presumably because they didn't have much hair, having transitioned late in life. Their style of dress, the way they applied makeup, the way they spoke: none of it worked for me. I wanted to empathise with them, having presumably much the same experience of gender dysphoria as them, but their life experience seemed so different to mine.

To compound my problems, the reactions of the cis people at the party didn't help. The party naturally started to split into factions. The trans people ended up in the dining room, the cis people were mostly in the lounge, with the kitchen populated by the younger, better-dressed cis women.

I was in the kitchen.

No matter how I felt my allegiances should be, I was socially a cis woman. I felt I was betraying the trans people.

"So how do you know Anne?"
"I work with her."
That was the typical opening line from most of the cis people I spoke to. It suggested they didn't know I was trans. It felt like I'd infiltrated the opposing camp. It didn't feel right.

I made an effort to bring the two groups together and brought some of my new kitchen-based cis women friends into the dining room in an attempt to mingle. If anything it just made it worse. One of the cis women said to a bewigged trans woman "Do you go out of the house dressed like that?"
"Of course I do. I work at the university."
I just cringed. The poor trans woman was clearly offended by the remarks. I said nothing but just stood and witnessed a very awkward clash of worlds.

My own perceptions were about to get challenged, as the questioning continued. It transpired that several of the trans women had wives. I realise now that sexual orientation and gender identity are two entirely different things, but back then the idea that there were lesbian trans women seemed quite a revelation. I'd honestly thought that all trans women were straight. In my naïve thinking, it seemed like a betrayal of one's female identity to fall in love with a woman. At that time, prior to the Gender Recognition Act, I was actually legally male and my only marriage option would have been to a woman, but I'd just accepted that trans people weren't permitted to marry in the UK.

What troubled me most about the party, and continued to haunt me for some time after, was that the tables had been turned on me and it made me very uncomfortable. I was a cis woman living out all the prejudices that I'd previously been subjected to. It was a horrible world to live in. I'd betrayed my sisters and I hated myself for it. I didn't socialise with Anne again, and once the contract at the customer site had ended I moved on and broke contact with her. At the most vulnerable time in her life, I'd ignored her. I was a bad person. I really didn't like myself.

My road-to-Damascus father's funeral experience changed me in many ways. One of the things I resolved to do was help my fellow trans people. I needed to right what I felt was a wrong I'd committed against Anne. I'd let myself be influenced by the superficial surface detail of how we perceive others. Never again would I be part of a society that shuns trans people because of how feminine or masculine or pretty they look. Our gender identity is not subject to the width of our shoulders or the density of the hair on our heads. We are beautiful people, all of us.

# Merry Christmas everyone

Here's a curious fact, and one I find hard to believe myself: since coming out to my family thirty years ago I have never spent Christmas Day with any members of my extended family. A family Christmas for me, the real me, has never existed. I really thought things would be different this year, after the death of my father, hoping that I could patch things up with my brother, but it wasn't to be. After receiving my first Christmas card in years from my brother last year, and having an initially promising meeting with him and his wife, things later descended into a text and email row about the need to keep me secret from his kids; I ended telling him to not bother until he stopped treating me as his dirty little secret. I haven't heard from him since.

Families, eh!?

Christmas is difficult for trans people: it throws the basic lack of understanding and support from our families into sharp relief. Some trans people have loving families who accept them unconditionally, some suffer complete rejection, others seem to maintain a surface gloss of acceptance until at Christmas the cracks show. A friend of mine, a post transition trans woman, was asked to dress male in order to avoid upsetting granny! My family split down the middle, with my parents and brother completely rejecting me, and the rest of my family completely accepting me. There are still cracks though, and come Christmas I'm asked to stay away, supposedly because of a lack of spare beds, maybe re-enacting the Christmas story of no room at the inn, but actually so that I don't bump into someone I'm not supposed to. I really thought it would be different this year.

Things were never easy for me at Christmas during my childhood. The groundwork was laid for future gender-based hostility early on. I learnt from an early age that wanting to dress as a Christmas fairy was not a good thing: mum's wedding dress, veil, and tiara were not play things for little boys! Then there was the doll incident. Despite all my early dressing up activities, *the doll incident* seemed to trouble my mum more than anything, such is the slavish adherence to gender stereotypes that society requires.

My mum had bought a doll for the neighbour's girl, and put it in the cupboard under the stairs until Christmas. I found the doll and was delighted. Finally my parents had bought me a Christmas present I really wanted, and I wouldn't let it go. After something of a battle, they finally had to take it by force with me blurting through a veil of tears "I want my dolly, I want my dolly!". Why were they so surprised when I finally came out as trans, years later?

I didn't fare too much better when it came to regular boy-gender-appropriate presents. My birthday is within two weeks of Christmas. They did make an effort to celebrate my birthday, and not start preparing for Christmas until after my birthday, but it seemed too much of a financial burden for most of my family. I'd often get hit with the line: "We haven't got you a birthday present this year, but we'll buy you an extra special present for Christmas". On Christmas Day I'd be unwrapping my presents with my brother and comparing the relative values of his presents with mine: there was no difference. I'd been stitched up yet again. Christmas is unfair!

My last ever family Christmas was 1982. Coming out as trans resulted in a brick wall of total rejection from my parents; I never went back home again. I tried to build a line of communication between them and the doctors at the Gender Identity Clinic, so that a dispassionate third party could explain that this was a medically recognised condition and not some lifestyle choice. The dispassionate third party eventually gave up and suggested it would be better for me to be left alone to transition, and my family obeyed.

My first few Christmases were spent with friends. I remember the first Christmas after transition I spent with the family of a close friend I worked with. I didn't realise at the time that she, along with all my other colleagues, had been briefed by the Ministry of Defence security people about me being trans, in order that I could be allowed to keep a lower level of security clearance after transition. When I tried to explain in vague terms about not going home for Christmas she seemed to understand and didn't press for more details; for this I was grateful, without understanding the extra information she was party to. It was a lovely day of celebration, in a lovely big house: her father being the boss of the company we worked for! I was given a great present which is still on my kitchen shelf to this day:

*Delia Smith's Complete Cookery Course.* Why would she think I couldn't cook? Aren't all girls taught cookery skills?

When the bombshell was dropped on me by the MoD that I wouldn't be permitted to work elsewhere in the defence industry without complete disclosure, the moment I finally realised all my friends and colleagues knew I was trans, I resolved to move to the south coast to further my windsurfing and leave the defence industry behind. I was set up on a date with Dougie, a local windsurfing retailer, and there then followed some of my happiest Christmases with the man I loved. Dougie didn't have the best of relationships with the rest of his family, and so we were ideally suited for Christmases by ourselves.

I think my favourite Christmas ever was Dougie and I on a British beach in the middle of winter in a freezing cold camper van. *The British do Christmas*! In the morning we windsurfed in three-foot waves: perfect for jumping and riding. At midday the wind dropped, so we retired to our camper van for turkey and cranberry sandwiches, mince pies, and Christmas crackers. We were pretty cold, but it's one of the best Christmases I've ever had!

By contrast, the following year was the worst Christmas I've ever had.

Ever since coming out to Dougie, our relationship had started to deteriorate, he started seeing someone else behind my back, and eventually he hit me with the "this isn't working" speech. He moved out two months before Christmas; I was heartbroken. That Christmas was the loneliest I'd ever spent. I spent much of Christmas Day walking the lanes around my house; I couldn't stay in the house on my own. I hadn't had any contact with anyone in my family for over eight years. I thought I could cope without them, but I was wrong. That Christmas sent me over the edge and into therapy. I was determined never to spend another Christmas alone.

Therapy was tough: talking about the difficulties with my parents was emotionally draining. I'd spend much of every session in floods of tears. I'd hoped to get advice about how best to try patching things up with my family, but it was clear that the rules were that advice was not to be given: we were to "reach conclusions jointly, by exploring your feelings". By the final session, I felt better, and we had reached the conclusion that I shouldn't contact my family.

Shortly afterwards, in contrast to the therapy conclusions, I contacted my Aunt.

To say the reaction of my Aunt on the other end of the phone was encouraging would be a massive understatement: she was overjoyed to hear from me. I'd always thought she was supportive: she seemed to understand me when I talked in guarded terms about gender and sexuality, even though I'd never come out to her. The sheer delight in her voice was wonderful. Shortly after that phone call, we had a reunion, and she instantly understood why I'd gone through transition: gone was the awkward shy boy, to be replaced by the rounded happy woman. I had my family back, or at least the half of my family that truly loved me.

I'd hoped that my Aunt would be able to act as a peacemaker between me and my parents, but they weren't going to budge: my mum seemed willing to have me back, but she was ruled by my father who was adamant he'd have nothing to do with me. My Aunt put me back in touch with my brother, but he too was not prepared to move forward: he'd told everyone he was an only child, and was unwilling to explain the sudden appearance of a sister to his wife's family. At least I had my Aunt, who treated me like her daughter. I wouldn't be alone next Christmas.

Next Christmas came, and I was alone once more. The problem with family Christmases is that family tend to turn up unannounced. As much as my Aunt loved me, I was still something of a dark family secret, or rather the fact that my Aunt was back in contact with me was a secret from my father: wherever he was, I couldn't be. I'd hoped that my Aunt would stand up for me, but she was trying to sail a course through the family divisions without upsetting anyone; I tried to sympathise, but it still hurt. The worst thing for me was when my cousins got married. Having been treated like a sister, I had hoped I would get to be bridesmaid, but I wasn't even invited to the weddings: once more I was left out in the cold in order to keep the rest of the family happy.

My Aunt does try to accommodate me in some way at Christmas, but this usually means us having a separate celebration: either my birthday before Christmas, or a New Year celebration. Either way, we have turkey and

Christmas pudding, and we do our best to make it a good substitute. It still doesn't quite feel the same as watching the Queen's speech with all your family gathered round on Christmas Day though.

I'm not unique in having family difficulties: some Irish friends of mine would spend their Christmases on their own, here in the UK, away from the rest of their family. I was invited to spend Christmas with them, and so it would continue for several years to come. I enjoyed our times together, and it became something of a tradition for the three of us to spend Christmas together. However, as previously mentioned, after casually outing myself on being asked about my tracheal shave scar, we never again spent Christmas together.

I am usually evasive when people ask about my plans for Christmas. It is a family time, and as much as I'd love to have an invitation to spend Christmas with friends, it wouldn't feel right for me trying to fit into someone else's family dynamic. I often need to explain to people why I can't spend Christmas with my own family, and usually give some examples of the blazing rows I had with my father. Many of these rows were unrelated to me being trans, and more connected with his constant need to control every aspect of my life. Those stories would offer a plausible explanation of why I couldn't be with my father. Explaining why I hadn't seen my brother in twenty years was a lot trickier: I tended to avoid such questions. I don't want to put myself in an environment where I'm having to explain my family divisions, without revealing the real reason I've been completely rejected by those closest to me. This lack of a back story is one of the difficult aspects of living life in stealth. I've always squirmed when talking about school days, particularly if the person knows my home town and asks which school I went to: I went to a boys' school!

It's now 2012 and I really thought this year would be different. My mother and father are dead and buried and no longer have to be factored into family plans. I was optimistic that relations with my brother would thaw and perhaps we could spend our first Christmas together, however he has still to come to terms with how to explain the sudden appearance of a sister to his family, and so I am still his dirty little secret. I had thought that finally I could spend Christmas Day with my Aunt, but she's in Germany visiting her son and his wife. I have started seeing someone, and was thinking maybe I could spend Christmas with him, but he's an entertainer and is hosting Christmas celebrations at local hotels all throughout the festive period.

Here I sit alone on Christmas Day, remembering all my Christmases past, and hoping that next year will be different. Merry Christmas everyone.

# The naked truth

I recently sent some very odd emails to a trans friend who was nervous about her imminent Gender Confirmation Surgery. They described me being naked in the changing rooms of the local leisure centre. I wanted to convey the comfort I felt in my body. I wanted her to see what a wonderful thing it was not to be ashamed of the body we'd been given. I hope she understood the intent of the emails, because sending messages about one being naked could be badly misconstrued!

I was born with a penis. It's not easy for me to write that. That piece of skin got me into a whole lot of trouble. The doctors took one look when I was born, and without a second's thought wrote 'boy', condemning me to a lifetime of problems. That thing has a lot to answer for.

I cross dressed secretly during my childhood, as many trans people do, but for me it wasn't always about the dresses and makeup. I would tuck the offending body part back between my legs and, with the assistance of an item of my mum's foundation-wear, could achieve a particularly smooth and female outline. I could wear my boy clothes in front of my family, concealing my female form underneath. I would lie on the couch reading, happy with my smooth outline, content. I don't think they ever knew I did this. It made me happy to pretend the source of my problems had gone away.

I hated being confronted with my male body. The showers at school were horrible: I couldn't stand anyone seeing me naked. I would avoid the showers wherever possible, which of course highlighted my discomfort to the other kids, and made the mockery even worse. This would make me even more self conscious, and so the cycle continued. Children can smell the fear, you know.

After the limbo period of my life during transition, surgery seemed to open up a world of possibilities, my body and mind now in harmony. For the first time since transition I could participate in sport; I could enjoy my body doing all manner of wonderful things. My first taste of my new found freedom came when a friend suggested we all go try windsurfing at a local lake. I now found myself standing in a changing room next to my best friend, having to change in front of her into my first ever swimming costume. I was nervous. I fumbled with the straps, and took two attempts to step into it correctly. I felt such a fool, but my friend didn't even notice. I later discovered she knew I was trans, but she never did anything to make me feel uncomfortable, or give any indication she regarded me as anything other than a regular woman.

My love of windsurfing took hold, and soon I was changing in cars, beach huts, on beaches, in sailing clubs, and toilets all over the country. I was now comfortable in my skin and it felt good. When I joined a running club, and starting entering races, I felt at ease in the changing rooms and communal showers at the various venues.

I noticed though, that not everyone is as comfortable in their skin as I was. While many of my friends, including me, are happy to hang their clothes up and walk naked to the showers, others make sure they stay covered in a large towel, careful to keep as much of their bodies covered as possible. Others take this to the extreme: at my local leisure centre we watched as a woman got into the shower fully clothed, draped a towel over the gap above the door, and hung her clothes over the door. Somehow she managed to shower without getting her clothes wet, but as she got dressed, still in the shower, she got too close to the touch sensitive shower control and gave herself a soaking. We found it funny, but I felt sorry for her. Surely I'm the one who should be body conscious, not her? There is of course a caveat: it is possible she was a pre-op trans woman, but I don't think so. She was young, and I think just exceptionally shy.

My body confidence was taken to its natural conclusion in those same changing rooms. I was using the gym while the main hall had been rented out to a lace fair. As you can imagine, the clientele of a lace fair are mostly older ladies. The entrance to the changing rooms is opposite the entrance to the main hall. The changing rooms do not have toilets - they are at the other end of the building. Thus there was a steady stream of little old ladies walking into the changing rooms, looking around enquiringly and then asking where the toilets were. I imagine most women of that age are unused to gym changing rooms; I know my mum had never done any sport in her life. I'd been cooling off from my gym session and drinking a sport drink before getting in the shower. At first I was happy to point everyone in the direction of the toilets, but I was beginning to tire of this. I'd just got undressed ready for the shower, when I heard the outer door open, and knew what was about to happen. I stood there, in the middle of the changing rooms, stark naked, waiting for the inevitable. In walked a frail-looking white-haired old lady. As she saw me, she took a sharp breath and let out a stifled scream; she was very shocked. She looked at me, said a quick "Sorry!", and turned round without enquiring about toilets. I was very wicked. It was fun!

It was those events I was trying to describe in the email to my friend as she waited, worried, for her surgery. Thinking back, that was a very strange email, but I was trying to show how far I'd come from the shy, ashamed youngster, to the bold brazen woman. It feels good to feel confident about my body.

I clearly have a strange sense of humour though: whenever I see a carton of Tropicana Smooth orange juice, I smile. It says on the side:
"Smooth. No bits."
I can't resist a smirk and thinking
"Yes, that's me!"

# Dilated to meet you

I have a vagina. God did not give me my vagina; he gave me a penis. Ha ha very funny. I bet you had a right good laugh about that, didn't you God? Thank you - not!

My vagina is man made. The man that made it was David Herbert. David Herbert was later struck off for malpractice. David Herbert was the man whose level of surgical aftercare was such that I took my own stitches out. David Herbert was the man who told me I could dilate with my fingers. David Herbert was the man who gave me hairs on the inside of my vagina. Ha ha, thank you God. You really do like a laugh don't you?

If you want details of my vaginoplasty then you're in the wrong place, switch off this book[16], and go do your own research: these are modern times and the information is out there. What I will say though, is they were not modern times when I had my surgery and what seemed acceptable then would be cause for accusations of malpractice today. Ah, yes...

To be fair to David Herbert, he was very keen to take my money, and offered me easy payment terms. I was almost bankrupting myself to have the surgery, and he let me pay in instalments. I was very grateful. He explained what was involved, explaining all the grisly details that you can nowadays lookup on the Internet. He failed though to explain the small issue of a hairy vagina.

If you've done your Internet research then you will now know that scrotal skin ends up repositioned to form labia and the outer part of the vagina. Scrotal skin is hairy, hence my problem. Perhaps I'm being harsh on the practices in 1986, because laser hair removal didn't exist back then. Diathermy and electrolysis did exist though, but there was no suggestion

---

[16] I'm assuming you're not so old fashioned as to be reading the paper version.

that I should have any sessions of it. A hairy vagina was apparently an acceptable outcome.

There's something of the spirit of the blitz amongst trans people; we're a tough bunch, having endured what would break many mortals. I described my insensitive, hairy, barely functioning vagina as *the best thing I ever did* to a friend who found this highly amusing; another friend was horrified at what she thought was abuse. Once the Internet had been invented, I was able to compare notes with other trans women and realised I was not alone. People just accepted that that was how things were for trans women. There were discussions about how to deforest a hairy vagina: one suggestion was to lube up with KY jelly and insert a tampon. One left the tampon in and waited for the lube to dry out, thus gluing the hairs to the tampon; a swift pull and you have a vaginal waxing. Ouch! Ooouuuch! I never tried that.

My surgical aftercare seemed to be an improvisational approach. After lectures about hygiene and salt baths, I was told about dilation: I would need to dilate both my vagina and my urethra. I imagined I was about to be given some amazing state of the art surgical instruments, a speculum on steroids, but no: after much rummaging I was given a syringe needle case to dilate my urethra, and told to use my fingers to dilate the vagina. I wondered at the time why no one was making a dilator for vaginoplasty surgery, but as there weren't that many of us, I figured there wasn't the demand to warrant the expense. I accepted the word of my surgeon. It never occurred to me that vaginal dilation is something many women, suffering for example from vaginismus or adhesions, have to do, and that dilators are commonly available.

I regret not talking dilation through with my GP at the time, but she didn't seem the friendliest type. She seemed to equate womanhood with breast size, and once criticised me for having small breasts. This was not someone with whom I felt comfortable discussing my vaginal width.

In the absence of proper medical advice I returned to my main source of information on the trans experience: my library of two trans biographies, Tula and April Ashley. April talked about the ritual humiliation she received at her divorce trial, where the lawyers attempted to prove she wasn't a woman capable of consummating a marriage. She talked of the requirement to be able to insert four fingers into the vagina as a prerequisite for accommodating a penis. This then became my benchmark: the four-finger shower crouch became my dilation routine.

It may seem ludicrous that I should take advice from a biography rather than go to my doctor, but I'd never felt accepted by the medical profession. My impression of my GP is that she wouldn't have time for mopping up after a cosmetic procedure simply for the purposes of having recreational sex. I didn't feel I'd be treated as a woman with a serious medical issue; her comment about my breast size seemed to confirm this. In fact my vaginal issues were fundamental to my sense of identity, as I was soon to discover.

An often heard benefit of being trans is that you get to lose your virginity twice. I was now thirty one, I'd been with Dougie three years, we were sleeping in the same bed but so far I'd managed to *keep* my virginity twice. We were three years into our relationship and Dougie was still unaware of my trans history. I felt the time had finally arrived and in the middle of some hot bed-based fumbling I uttered the line:
"There's something I need to tell you first."
That is not the best precursor to sex.

This was a huge moment in my life. I loved Dougie very much, and I was so afraid of the consequences of my disclosure. I'd cut myself off from everybody who knew I was trans, and for six years I'd lived a life of total stealth. Being trans just didn't enter into my daily life, but deep down the secret lurked: something I'd been made to feel ashamed of from my earliest years. I was crying before I'd even told Dougie why. It felt like I was tearing my soul out in front of him. He took it well though, but like I said, not the best precursor for sex.

We continued though, on what could have been the best night of my life.

The sex was traumatic.

The sex was painful.

It destroyed our relationship.

With hindsight, we should have talked my problems through and I should have sought help from the doctor. Instead, I lost all my confidence. I felt like I'd had my femininity taken away from me: I'd failed at a fundamental level.

Dougie and I stayed together for another two years, but it was downhill from that point onwards. I felt deeply ashamed, and I don't think Dougie felt it was something he could talk through with me. The one time soon after that night that he broached the subject, I again ended up in floods of tears.

Eventually I heard the words "I don't think this is working" and thus began the loneliest year of my life.

A year of reflection and therapy did result in me contacting my Aunt and Uncle, who were delighted to welcome me back into the family, so some good came of the breakup. I never talked to anyone though of the problems I'd had with Dougie, and so began twenty years of celibacy.

I opened this account of my life with a description of my father's funeral. It took such an event to make me reappraise my life and make me feel proud of who I am. I finally had a feeling of self worth and the drive to fix the problem. I booked laser sessions at a specialist clinic to address my intimate hair issues. I discovered that one could buy all manner of different dilators online and I started dilating properly.

Why did it take me so long to get there?

I had no confidence dealing with the medical profession. I'd never had a positive experience revealing my trans status to a doctor. When I finally plucked up the courage to talk about dilation with my new GP, although he was very sweet and wanted to help, he had no idea how to deal with me and wanted to send me back to Charing Cross Hospital eighty miles away. I was his only trans patient. It is usually the case that when a trans person goes to the doctor with a trans related issue, the patient usually knows more than the doctor. This time around I was able to get all the information I needed from other trans women online. Back in the early nineties I didn't have that option and felt very isolated and alone: I shut myself off and tried to put my problems to the back of my mind.

I regret not talking things through with Dougie and seeking help; maybe we would still be together if I had.

Us trans folk are a tough bunch. It helps to have a sense of humour about these things. I can't help giggle when I hear Joan Rivers' old gynaecologist routine:
"Dr Schwartz, at your cervix. Dilated to meet you".

# Boobs

I recently had one of my first entirely positive experiences of health care. I've not had a great track record with doctors and hospitals, so it was good to come away from a hospital visit feeling better for the experience. What was this life affirming experience? I had my first mammogram.

I was quite surprised at how soon after my fiftieth birthday the breast screening letter arrived. I was now on the three year cycle of mammograms that would continue until I was seventy[17]. While some women might baulk at the idea of a breast exam, I welcomed the idea, not simply because screening programmes are a fundamentally sensible idea, but because it felt like I was reclaiming some lost birthright; this was a uniquely female experience.

This was one time I felt there was no need to out myself. I've always worried over the consequences of outing myself to medical staff; you'd think they are professional people who would treat you with respect and dignity, but this has not always been the case. I've had my share of bad treatment over the years, and it all started at the very place which should have been supportive of me: Charing Cross Hospital.

I was attending my first appointment at the Gender Identity Clinic at Charing Cross in London. I was aware of the need to impress, and show my trans credentials so I was dressed up smartly in a black skirt and red batwing jumper. (As always in emotionally charged memories, I can see myself, and what I was wearing.) I had yet to be prescribed hormones, this being my first visit, but was quite passably female. I hoped that this would be the moment I got my hands on hormones, but before they could

---

[17] I asked the radiographer why the screening stops at seventy. She replied that even if you get breast cancer at seventy, it's far more likely something else will kill you first!

prescribe anything I had to have a blood test, so I was sent downstairs to the phlebotomy department.

I waited patiently and when my time came I was asked to sit in the chair in the middle of the room and roll up my sleeve. The nurse politely took my yellow slip of paper, and started getting herself organised, sorting my paperwork out. She came over and sat down next to me, and as she read my details her mood changed dramatically: she looked really angry. She shouted at me:
"Oh my god, you're one of them! Why didn't you say something? You've just wasted my time."
She stormed off.

I was taken aback! What did she mean? Why had I wasted her time? I had no doubt that she was referring to the fact that I was trans, or presumably to her way of thinking *a man*, but why would that make a difference to a blood test? I got my answer a few minutes later when she returned wearing some form of biological contamination suit. This was 1984, and while George Orwell's vision of his future may not have been particularly accurate, to people working with blood, the world was a scary place due to Acquired Immunodeficiency Syndrome, AIDS. She regarded me, *a nasty tranny*[18] in her eyes, as a high AIDS risk. I was in fact a virgin and had never even kissed anybody romantically, so was probably the lowest risk in the entire hospital. It was so humiliating. No one should ever be treated with such lack of respect. She made me feel worthless. I'd come to Charing Cross to seek help for a condition that had given me terribly low self esteem, and she'd just crushed me. I managed to avoid crying, but only just.

I somehow got myself together for the subsequent interview with the psychiatrist, but didn't mention anything about the blood incident; I didn't want to rock the boat. My life literally depended on the outcome of the interview and I wanted to say all the right things. Fortunately everything went well, and by the next interview I'd been prescribed the hormones and testosterone blockers that I so badly wanted. All was well or so I thought;

---

[18] *Tranny* is highly derogative. It is the trans community's n- word. Please don't ever refer to someone as a tranny.

little did I know that behind the scenes the doctors had told my family to break all contact with me[19].

I had something of a mistrust of doctors and nurses from that point onwards, but always felt I had a duty to disclose being trans when presenting for treatment. Over the years this attitude was to get revised somewhat.

At the height of my windsurfing career I awoke one morning with breathing difficulties and was admitted to hospital with a pneumothorax: a collapsed lung. There was no apparent reason for the collapse, other than the strenuous training I was doing at the time, hence it was termed a *spontaneous pneumothorax*. I felt that perhaps being trans was relevant to the diagnosis, so I freely volunteered this information to the consultant. The information seemed to come as quite a shock to him, but he said nothing, and I had no reason to suspect any problem. Later, I heard him talking about me to one of the nurses, just inside the door to my room; he didn't seem concerned whether I could hear him or not, but he wasn't talking directly to me. I listened to him describe how they needed to use a pump to assist the chest drain, as my lung was not re-inflating as expected: "You'll need to attach the pump to *his* chest drain."
My heart sank. I hoped I'd misheard, but he then used the word *him* to describe me.

Maybe I don't need to point out the obvious, but using the wrong pronouns to describe a trans person is incredibly rude and disrespectful. I was absolutely seething, but he was gone before I could say anything. I let my anger fester inside me. It ruined my stay in hospital and made me wary of medical staff from then on. When I next saw the consultant, a few days later, I didn't talk about his misdemeanour; I have deep regret that I said nothing. Nowadays I will always call out situations where I see myself or

---

[19] I only found out many years later that to resolve the conflict between me and my family, the psychiatrist had advised them to cut contact with me and allow me to transition in peace, and alone.

other trans people being disrespected; back then I didn't want to cause a fuss.

My policy from then on was to not disclose to medical staff. This maybe backfired on me after my lung collapsed a second time. I spent another week in hospital, a different hospital this time, and they managed to get me patched up by use of a chest drain to re-inflate the lung just as before. I did not disclose to anyone during my stay. The doctors suspected there might be an underlying cause, so sent me to a chest specialist. Again, I didn't disclose I was trans. After examining me, the doctor suspected I might have *Marfan Syndrome* based on the following observations:
- I had suffered recurring spontaneous pneumothorax
- My wingspan from finger tip to finger tip was 4" greater than my height
- At 5' 10" I was very tall
- I had a high palette

I took the last point to mean that my face was unusually elongated. It was explained to me that Marfan Syndrome is a genetic weakness in the connective tissue that can cause lung problems, resulting in pneumothorax, and more critically, a weakness in the aorta which can lead to a rupture, which is usually fatal. It was suggested I went for an echocardiogram to check for an enlarged heart and aorta and hopefully rule out Marfan; I duly obliged, and was given the all clear.

It didn't occur to me at the time, but the diagnosis might have been different if he'd known I was trans. I'm tall, but not that tall for a trans woman. My high palette may also be attributed to me being trans. I don't think my wingspan is necessarily attributable to me being trans, as it's more a general indication of a certain body type with long limbs, however I remember him mentioning my long fingers, which I think was his polite way of saying I had quite large hands: a Marfan symptom in a cis woman, but not necessarily in a trans woman. I was given the all-clear as regards Marfan Syndrome, but I may have clouded the diagnosis by withholding information.

I am still reluctant to disclose to medical staff. My policy is to answer all questions truthfully, but if they don't ask, I don't divulge. This can lead to some interesting discussions around medication and menstruation. A recent conversation with a nurse prior to a foot operation went like this:

"Are you on medication?"

"HRT"

"Ooh, have you had a hysterectomy?"

(I'm assuming she thought I was too young to be menopausal, or maybe she saw the brand of HRT on my form and knew it wasn't usually prescribed for menopause.)

"I had Sex Reassignment Surgery in my early twenties"

(Why didn't I say vaginoplasty? I don't like the terms SRS, GRS[20] or GCS[21].)

"So do you have periods?"

"No"

"Have you ever had periods?"

"No"

"Is there any chance you're pregnant?"

"No"

She was very sweet, but I'm not quite sure she fully understood what I was saying.

A few months later I was re-admitted to have my other foot operated on. I had to fill in the same forms, and this time I put *amenorrhea*[22] on the form where it asked for date of last period. As before a nurse went through my answers, saw my answer for date of last period and asked:

"So when *was* the date of your last period?"

"I've never had a period"

"So is there any chance you're pregnant?"

"None"

"Ok. We'll have to get you to sign a disclaimer to state there's no chance you're pregnant. Is that ok?"

"Yes"

Under the circumstances, I regarded that as a successful conclusion.

---

[20] Gender Reassignment Surgery, or Genital Reconstruction Surgery
[21] Gender Confirmation Surgery
[22] Absence of menstruation

I then had the anaesthetist to deal with.
"Have you had any major operations?"
"I've had some minor ones such as varicose veins and wisdom tooth, but the big one was a pleurectomy[23]."
"Any others?"
I'd hoped he'd be happy with just those!
"I had a vaginoplasty in my early twenties."
He was clearly taken aback.
"Well it takes all sorts!... Erm... er...I'm ok with that!"
His reaction bothered me. I was about to put my life in his hands. For the sake of his career and my life, I'd bloody well hope he was *ok with that,* even if I was Bertie Bassett[24].

I wondered if I was over-reacting to his response, so at my two-week checkup with the surgeon, who knew I was trans and had been completely professional and courteous towards me, I told him what the anaesthetist had said. The surgeon's sudden sharp intake of breath confirmed that I wasn't over-reacting. I explained that his attitude might offend other trans people, and I felt he should have a think about how he'd reacted and how that might come across. The surgeon said he'd have a word with him, but that he felt I'd knocked the anaesthetist off his theatrical stride, and that he wouldn't have intended any offence. The surgeon said I could make a formal complaint if I wanted, but I just wanted to gently call out his behaviour. At my next checkup I learnt that the anaesthetist had been completely mortified to hear that I'd been concerned about his reaction. I'd made my point, so job done, and hopefully he'll be a little more tactful next time.

So here I am in a waiting room with other ladies of a certain age, waiting for my first mammogram. I'm waiting for a uniquely female right of passage. I'm about to have my prized possessions checked: my pride and joy - my boobs.

---

[23] The pleurectomy was to prevent further lung collapses: the chest lining is removed, which sticks the lung to the chest wall.
[24] The mascot for Bassett's Liquorice All Sorts

You may detect that I am most proud of my lovely shirt potatoes. They may be small and humble, so that Shakira wouldn't confuse them with mountains, but they are B cups, and more than adequate. They are all my own work, entirely home grown; they are my own flesh and blood, with not a drop of silicone contained within. They are the main thing about my body which is authentically and undeniably female. I love Danny and Arnold[25], my lovely sweater stretchers.

My name is called and I go through the door marked with a propeller, warning of the presence of X-rays. I strip to the waist, and happily point out my chest drain and pleurectomy scars to the radiographer, when asked about operations, as if to emphasise that they are not there as a result of a boob job. She assures me that the pleurectomy scars around my right shoulder blade are now barely visible, and I am led to the X-ray machine. She expertly positions my boob on the plate of the machine without actually touching my boob; to be honest I wouldn't have cared if she'd grabbed my boob and led me to the machine by it, but not everyone is as carefree about their naked bodies as I seem to have become.

The next part is the bit that some women are not very keen on: she warns me that it might be a little uncomfortable, as the upper plate automatically lowers to squash my boob between the two plates as the X-ray is taken. It is a rather odd sensation, but it doesn't bother me in the slightest. A second shot is taken with the plate rotated 90°, and the process repeated on Arnold. I get dressed and we are done.

I can't stress enough how life affirming it all felt. It came almost as a shock, when she told me I'd receive the results within a fortnight and be hopefully given the all-clear: I needed reminding of the serious purpose behind the test. I do not know if there are stats concerning the incidence of breast cancer in trans women, to know if I run an increased risk. I take Premarin, an œstrogen sourced from pregnant mares which is less favoured these

---

[25] They are Twins, but Danny is nearer the ground than Arnold

days compared to synthetic œstrogens, and have my blood pressure tested regularly due to a risk of hypertension, but there does not appear to be an increased risk of breast cancer from what I've been told. I personally have had no health concerns regarding my medication, and I wasn't particularly concerned about the result of the mammogram, but it was good nonetheless when a short while later I received my negative result.

The sad fact remains that my mammogram is the one time I felt completely at ease during a visit to a hospital; being trans can give a very different perspective on healthcare.

# Stereotypes

I recently had an argument with my aunt concerning the wearing of female clothes and makeup. This was not however the typical troubles of a trans woman and her family's perceptions of her gender expression; my aunt loves me dearly, and completely supports me. The argument was about the fact that I often wore jeans and no makeup when I visited her.

Her daughter, my cousin, is at the far end of the girlie spectrum. She has a separate room in her country mansion for her shoes and handbags. I kid you not! You will rarely see her out of makeup. It is against this background that my femininity is judged.

I am female.

I just thought I'd give that its own paragraph. It's not up for debate. My aunt however gets confused between my gender and my femininity.

I've given in to her.

I enjoy looking nice. I like getting made-up and dressed-up for a night out. I love looking smart and sassy at work. I don't however think it defines me. For some peace of mind though, I now make sure I dress a shade more feminine when I go home for the weekend.

This isn't the first time I've adapted my gender expression for others. I came out to my best friend just prior to transition, and she didn't take it well. She felt my femininity and gender identity were somehow fake. At the time, the early 80s, I enjoyed playing video games on pub consoles and my BBC B computer. Her take:
"You know that's a very male thing - women don't play video games."

I so needed her acceptance, I haven't played a video game since. (If you see me playing Angry Birds on my iPhone, I will deny all knowledge).

My new man, after three dates and prior to me disclosing my trans history, said "Wow, that's so unusual for a woman to like Star Trek". Why is scifi so popular amongst trans women? Are young girls pressured to not like scifi, as it's boy-stuff, and we've escaped the conditioning? I feel no pressure to conform - is it really so unusual for women to like scifi? I enjoy a good chick flick as much as anyone else, but my favourite movie of all time is Lana ( and Andy ) Wachowski's *The Matrix*. What a fantastic day it was when my hero Lana went public on being trans - what a great role model she is.

I make electronic music and have a love of synthesisers, particularly the classic 70s and 80s pre-digital synths. The old classics have such a warmth and character, that was absent from many of the later digital-age keyboards. I've amassed quite a collection of synths, including my cherished Minimoog, the classic of classics. I'm rather geeky when it comes to all-things-synth: is it wrong that I know that R2D2's voice was created using an ARP 2600 synthesiser? - a synth I hope one day to own.

I've met some fellow electronic musicians through social networking, and they are mostly male, although there are a small number of women electronic musicians and producers. One of the guys commented to me: "It's so unusual to meet a woman who has more synths than I do". I won't deny I'm a rare breed, but why shouldn't a woman indulge her passion for something slightly off norm? The 70s and 80s were hugely influential decades for me, and I witnessed the birth of electronic music at a time when I had no money to own any of the new technology; what money I had was being saved up for my surgery. Now, in my later years, I have the resources to relive something that was denied me.

A trans female friend once told me "I used to be into synths". I didn't question her further on that statement, but I took it to mean she moved on after transition. Hormones have a huge influence on one's emotional state: for example I really don't have any desire to play video games anymore and find them boring. My friend's focus in life may well have changed, but I wondered if she somehow felt it wasn't a particularly feminine thing to have a passion for synths.

I'm a feminist; I'd hope most women are. Trans women get a hard time from the more radical end of feminism: where feminists are trying to break down society's sexist view of how women should look and act, trans women seem to just reinforce the gender stereotypes. I agree wholeheartedly that we should be challenging society's expectations of women's behaviour, but I would ask that critics of trans women take a walk in our shoes first, no matter how high the heels.

I would love nothing more than to wear jeans, t-shirt, comfy shoes and not bother with makeup: it would save me a fair bit of precious time getting ready. My sporting activities are not compatible with getting dolled up, although I do see women at the gym in designer gear and makeup and I confess it makes me cringe. I would love nothing more than to roll out of bed, slip on some slobby clothes, go grab a newspaper from the local shop and be greeted with "Good morning madam, rough night?". The reality though, is I would likely hear "That's £1.40 sir". That's not something a cisgender woman ever has to worry about.

Being misgendered is a mercifully rare event for me these days, and I really hope to keep it that way. I have my sloppy no-makeup days, but if I'm going out and interacting with people I like to leave no doubt as to my gender. Being misgendered still hurts, even after twenty eight years of taking the blows. My defence against those low punches is my body armour: feminine clothes, long hair and makeup.

I represented Great Britain internationally at windsurfing and tried to show the public what a *real* windsurfing woman looked like: not the models draped over the boards in the sexist adverts, who wouldn't have a clue as to the difference between the luff and the clew, but the small band of dedicated passionate women in a sport dominated by men. I was never pretty enough to get my face in a magazine, but at least my results did get reported on, if only to have a barely discernible photo of me out at sea and the caption "Occasional flashes of brilliance". I was out there trying to get the voice of women heard in a very sexist sport.

I do the things I like to do. I watch scifi, superhero and horror movies. I've decided that I don't really get the whole computer games thing after all, and I use my high-spec computer for music production and 3D modelling.

I love the macho sport of windsurfing, but have no time for football, rugby or cricket. The thought of me playing football or rugby fills me with horror, but I will passionately defend the right of any woman to play those sports.

So I like to get glammed up and look nice for my man? Well sue me.

# Marathon girl

I think I have an obsessive-compulsive side to my personality. I've never had problems with addiction: I don't drink to excess, I don't take drugs, and I never gamble. However, I tend to get drawn into things and have to know all about them. I study, I think, I analyse; I can get quite obsessed. I take up windsurfing: I get to the world championships. I take up running: I get to elite level...

...well nearly!

After retiring from windsurfing I needed a way to stay in shape. I'd always done a little bit of running as part of my windsurfing training, so when a friend suggested I join her running club, I thought I'd give it a go.

It could have been something of a come down from being at the top of a sport to being at the very bottom, but it was fun: I was very much the slowest runner in the club, and I was participating for the pure joy of running. All the strength I'd gained from windsurfing counted for nothing in endurance running; I was a complete beginner and loving the lack of both pressure and very expensive equipment.

I was glad to be the slowest. I'd always had a nagging doubt that I wasn't competing fairly: that being trans gave me an advantage over the other women. At the time, I was banned from the Olympics, and I'd imagined that must be for good reason. However, all my experience had suggested that I was no different to any other woman in sport, and in fact I was now starting to see that I might have a disadvantage in running, with my more male skeleton and female musculature giving me a power to weight disadvantage. It was with much relief I heard the news that the ban had been lifted at the Sydney Olympics: it validated me testing myself against my female friends.

Everyone was so much faster than me; I was always right at the back of the field. It used to frustrate me immensely that it took me so long to jog out to our training venues that they would start the session before I got there, such was their unwillingness to wait for me to arrive. I'd often have to miss half of the stretching routine due to my tardiness. (Now that I'm qualified as a coach I should say that nowadays, stretching before a session, even if properly warmed up, is frowned upon, and dynamic mobility exercises, or drills, are preferred.)

I noticed how much faster the men were than the women. This might seem an obvious statement, but I expected there to be much more of an overlap. I expected to see fast women up with the lead men and the slowest men at the back with the women, but there seemed to be a big gulf between the men and women with only one or two of the faster women crossing the gap. While in some ways it was comforting that I was the slowest, I was determined to improve; I wanted a place at the front of the pack.

I've since learnt why there is this apparent gulf between the recreational male and female runners: men train harder. At elite and good-standard club level, men generally have a 10% performance advantage over women, all other things being equal. The advantage is the extra strength that testosterone gives. At recreational level though, all things are not equal, and testosterone gives another advantage other than strength: men are more driven, and simply train harder. The men in my club are always testing themselves against each other, trying to be top dog, if only for that particular session. We women have a completely different approach to training sessions, being more social and supportive, and are more likely to slow down to let others catch up, than to try to be the first back. One of the lessons I needed to learn when I later took up coaching was that some women don't want to train like they are on their way to the top, and that's ok: enjoying your sport is by far the most important goal before we start to consider performance-related aspects.

I'd never thought that windsurfing was the best sport for a trans woman in terms of body shape: you end up with big shoulders, which is not a good look if you are already have a large frame. Running seemed a much better fit, particularly endurance running, with less muscle bulk in the upper body. I liked what running was doing to my figure.

I was entering local races and getting a taste for longer distances. What had seemed an impossibility when I started was now just another target in my journey towards speed and fitness. I started to dare think that I could try for the ultimate challenge: I wanted to do the London Marathon.

The London Marathon is heavily oversubscribed: entries go into a ballot and places are allocated to the lucky few. The consensus at the time was that there was a one in four chance of getting a place. I sent off my entry, but didn't realistically expect to get in. I imagined that I would carry on building up my training and when eventually I got lucky then I would have built a much firmer base of fitness to do the specific marathon work on top. I was quite shocked then, when I got a place at the first attempt. My club mates were equally shocked: the slowest runner in the club was about to do a marathon!

I found a schedule in a magazine and stuck to it. A feature of training for a spring marathon such as London is that you are training right through the winter. It's cold, it can be wet, it can blow horizontal hail at you so that you pull your wooly hat right over your face to ease the pain, but I didn't miss a run. On my kitchen wall was pinned my schedule and I'd tick each run off as if I was running my foes through one by one. My biggest foe apart from the marathon itself was the dreaded twenty mile run: for me this would be the Worthing 20, three weeks before London.

Worthing gave me my first feeling of what running a marathon might be like. I was so nervous beforehand, having never run the distance before, but having everyone else around made it so much easier: both my fellow runners, and the small number of supporters at the roadside cheering us on. I got such a lift from those around me; what had initially seemed so daunting was becoming just another training run. I crossed the finishing line with a sense of fulfilment, not because I'd just completed my first twenty mile run, but because of the realisation that I'd just completed the last big challenge of my schedule: I was now ready for the London Marathon.

With three weeks remaining, another challenge arose: getting sponsorship money. I wasn't obliged to raise money, as this was my own marathon entry and not a charity golden bond place. There's a whole industry around golden bond entries: around half the places are sold to charities and then the charities sell them on in exchange for a pledge to raise a minimum amount for the charity, often in excess of £2000. I chose to run for Parkinson's UK. My club mates were all willing to sponsor me, but wanted to set a target time. Was just finishing not enough for them? Welcome to the world of competitive athletics. I chose a time of 4 hours 30 minutes, which surprised many: *so the club's slowest runner was going to run a marathon in 4:30 was she? Yeah right!*

Honk!! The time had flown by and we were there! The culmination of fourteen weeks of focused effort. I was running the London, sorry, *Flora* London Marathon. At least I *thought* I was running the Flora London Marathon: that honk was just a faint distant impression of the starting signal and in an underwhelming non-event of a start we just stood around to various shouts of "has it started?". We didn't have to worry too much about wasted time as we were individually timed with chips on our shoes once we crossed the start line, which after ten minutes of shuffling we finally achieved.

The first mile was a start stop affair as we waited for the mass of runners to thin out. Just as running was starting to get a bit smoother I got barged out of the way by a woman shouting "Excuse me, I've got to follow the balloons!". She was trying to follow the 4 hours 30 minutes pacer and was clearly not that relaxed about it. I wonder if she realised all the other runners around her, including me, were also doing the same thing? I decided that being in the vicinity of the pace group might prove a little crowded so I ran on ahead at my own, slightly quicker, pace.

We went past a short section of open ground with a wall running down the side of it, and there was a line of maybe a dozen men all facing the wall with their hands together. Unless it was a religious meeting, I assume they couldn't be bothered to queue patiently for the toilets before the race like us girls. Really boys, have some dignity! It's at times like that, that I am proud to be a woman.

The mood was light and jovial as we eased ourselves into the race, but that was soon to change as we came across a big hairy guy in a fairy costume being given CPR by the medics at the roadside. The potential tragedy was thrown into sharp relief by the incongruous sight of the hairy fairy lying there. We later learnt that it had been a fatality, a not uncommon event at the London Marathon, and some people were quite upset about this. There were of course press stories about the dangers of marathon running, but it's a simple fact that if you have a heart problem then you are more likely going to find out during sport than sitting in front of the television; it doesn't mean running is dangerous.

That event had a strong resonance for me. Some years earlier when I first joined the club, I was running a long distance relay event in the countryside and my friend and team mate had a heart attack. I was the first to get to him, or rather the first who was prepared to assist him, as, almost criminally, several other runners had passed him without offering assistance. I was giving him CPR for over thirty minutes as the ambulance couldn't find us. I couldn't save him. It took me a long time to get over that tragedy, not because I blamed myself as such, but more through anger that no one administered CPR earlier, and it was left to me and my team mates arriving minutes later to actually do something. Years later I had a chance conversation with a paramedic who was a regular at the Great South Run. He told me that he'd attended several heart attack victims at the finish line and had got to them with a mechanical ventilator and defibrillator almost the moment they hit the ground. He had never saved anyone. He explained that the body is in such oxygen debt due to the exertion that it's almost impossible to supply the demand by artificial means. I could not have saved my friend, and equally tragically our hairy fairy was doomed the moment his heart gave up.

Back with the marathon, after maybe 9 miles came the announcement that my idol Paula Radcliffe had beaten the world record by *%$&!£*@5 seconds. No one around me could hear the time because as soon as the words "Paula Radcliffe has beaten the wor...", all the runners and spectators were cheering so loudly. I discovered later that she had totally destroyed the old record, knocking minutes off it and establishing the record that stands to this day: 2 hours 15 minutes 25 seconds. That is one of the most incredible runs of all time and in percentage terms far outstrips any of Usain Bolt's world records. I will stick my neck out and say that as you are reading this, that record will still have not been broken. I would imagine it will be decades before anyone gets close to it. Paula was not only fastest woman that day, but she also took the British men's title, as no British man ran faster. While that is utter brilliance on Paula's part, it's a sad indictment of the state of British men's endurance running, in the days before Mo Farah.

As we passed a road sign which said "Urban Clearway - No stopping under any circumstances", it started getting very crowded again as people stopped by the road side for a rest. Couldn't anybody read?! I heard a voice behind shouting "Rhino coming through!". He clearly didn't like being held up! Why couldn't I shout "Trans woman in first marathon coming through!"? It's not fair. As the rhino caught me, the road got even more crowded: this was *the rhino effect*. The cameras were bound to pick out the rhino at some point, so everyone was sticking with the rhino to get their faces on TV. Once I realised this I pushed on to overtake him, only to find the same problem with a giant Taylor's port bottle. The crowd were shouting "Come on bottle!". I also overtook the following: a womble, a watch, a giraffe, Spiderman in Lycra, Spiderman in cotton, a Mister Man, a clown, Noddy (but no Big Ears), several fairies, the Incredible Hulk (more like the incredible twiglet - he was painted green anyway) and naked fig-leaf man (flesh coloured shorts, lots of fake tan and a Tina Turner wig).

It was starting to get damn hot, and with the combination of heat, fatigue and the slowing of the crowds of runners around me my pace had dropped right off. What had seemed like an easy target of 4 hours 30 minutes was now looking more challenging. I got a timely boost from the Parkinson's supporters station; the crowd really do help, but they can also hinder. Spectators had been dashing across the course at regular intervals; I'd seen some near misses but nothing serious so far. I then saw an act of astonishing stupidity: a woman sauntered straight out in front of me, pushing a bicycle. I had enough time to alter course and not be impeded, but the old guy next to me had to swerve and caught his foot on the rear wheel causing him to fall. He got up and carried on, but looked to be in extreme pain; her stupidity had likely just robbed someone of his dream. It was my turn for an encounter as we passed the Tower of London: a couple of spectators holding hands - so sweet, and all the better for catching runners - ran straight into me. I hit them head on so didn't stumble and didn't hurt myself. I knocked one of them to the ground. Lesson learnt?

My lesson was being learnt as we entered the last six miles: the marathon is a pleasant steady run of 18 to 20 miles, in the company of happy like-minded people, followed by 6 miles of hell where each step seems a challenge. My left hip was so painful; I'd never experienced this in training. My muscles were all tightening up and my hip bone had decide to play my iliotibial band like a banjo string. I wanted to stop. I so desperately wanted to stop. I was playing mind games between the two halves of my brain in a battle to win control of my legs. The battle with time was being lost though. As Big Ben loomed into view it told me what I already knew from the clocks at the roadside: I was not going to achieve 4:30.

Despite my fatigue, I managed a flourish as we went past Buckingham Palace to view the finish line 300m down the Mall. Pain was cast aside as I sprinted for all I was worth, with tears flowing down my face. I got into a sprint battle with various guys I passed, beating some, losing to others, as we all tried to give that little extra for the benefit of the crowds, the cameras and our egos. I was timed at 4 hours 34 minutes. Smile for the finish line camera and we're done: that should be a nice one for the album.

I hated my photos.

Amidst the euphoria of completing my first marathon and all the plaudits from my friends, there was the discomfort of seeing quite a masculine looking me staring out of the official photos. For one thing I looked quite chunky, having put on twenty pounds since my windsurfing days. Seeing myself at my dishevelled worst though, with hair plastered down with sweat and distressed drawn features, just seemed to strip away what female attributes I had. I really hated those photos. It was like I'd outed myself to all the viewers of the London Marathon photo website.

That was the moment the decision was made: I booked in for Facial Feminisation Surgery.

The marathon bug had bitten and I knew I had to have more agony and ecstasy in my life. I applied again for London, and against the odds I got in. My facial surgery was going to have to be planned around the marathon. The date for the surgery was set for a week after the marathon: no interruption in training and a perfect time for a break before setting my sights on getting some nice looking finish line photos in the next marathon.

My training progressed well but I hadn't bargained for what I was told at my facial surgery consultation: I was going to have to come off HRT a month before the operation. I was going to have to do my final preparations and the marathon itself during full menopause symptoms!

I didn't really know what to expect. I'd had some strange experiences before my vaginoplasty surgery having come off my medication then, although they weren't menopause symptoms. I had been taking blocker drugs to stop the effects of my body's own testosterone, so rather than suddenly being hit by a complete lack of sex hormones, I suddenly had œstrogen replaced by testosterone. The results were alarming, but not quite what I'd expected: a week or so after stopping my meds I felt a damp patch on my front and was at first confused as to where it was coming from. I then realised with horror that I was lactating. I say horror, because I found it rather embarrassing to have this happen in front of friends who I thought didn't know I was trans. After the initial shock though I found a strange comfort in knowing that my breasts did in fact work!

I had no idea what menopause symptoms would feel like, but it didn't take too long to find out: the hot flushes started after only a few days. I'd be sitting at my desk and suddenly feel hot and exhausted. My face would go bright pink and I'd feel incredibly uncomfortable, like my head was going to explode. The tissue supply on my desk was getting used up mopping the sweat from my armpits.

This was nothing compared to what soon started happening at night. I guess I can't say whether my face was bright pink as it would kick in while I was sleeping, but I would be woken up in the small hours to the aftermath of my hot flush. I would wake up with the bed sheets soaking wet, the sweat coming mostly from a triangular area from my collarbone down to the bottom of my ribs. Between my breasts would be a river of sweat. Unlike the hot sweat of exercise, this seemed to be a cold sweat. I can't say whether I was hot to begin with, but by the time I awoke, I was a cold clammy mess in need of a towelling down. Oh god, bring back my œstrogen.

I felt tired and irritable and really didn't want to train, but actually the training seemed to help: it seemed to level me and lessen the symptoms. What initially had felt like an overwhelming challenge, now seemed like it might be the one thing I could do that wasn't affected by menopause.

Marathon day arrived and I felt ready. Once again I was raising money for Parkinson's and my club mates had demanded a target of 4 hours: double sponsorship for breaking the 4 hour barrier. The marathon played out in a similar fashion to the previous year with my target seeming in the bag until those hellish last few miles. I was proud of the fact that I ran the whole way, never stopping for a rest even at the water stations, but still the target defeated me. I had however knocked a full 30 minutes off the previous year, to bring me in at a menopausal 4 hours 5 minutes.

Still though, I hated my finish-line photos.

The solution to my body image issue was at hand though, as a few days later I was admitted for my facial surgery. A few weeks later I was back in training with my new female face, back on my œstrogen, and looking forward to new challenges.

I couldn't believe my luck in getting through the London Marathon ballot for a third time in a row. This time I had a more concrete target: I wanted to get under 3:45 as this was the *Good For Age* target. If you had run a marathon in the last two years faster than 3:45 then you were guaranteed a place in the London Marathon: no more testing my luck with the ballot.

As was becoming customary with my targets, I missed again, this time by just two minutes. I was getting faster though.

I did however have two rather nice bonuses: I won an online competition to win a Nike running vest signed by my hero Paula Radcliffe. The biggest bonus however was I now had finish-line photos I could be proud of. I had been steadily stripping down the extra weight to reveal a newly athletic body, which went well with my newly sculpted face. In my photos I looked every inch the female athlete I knew myself to be. Hanging in my hallway is a large frame, with my medal and photo to one side, Paula's finish-line photo to the other side, and in the middle a Nike top with the marker pen inscription:
"To Anne, congratulations on your 3:47 in London. Best wishes Paula Radcliffe 2:17"

Still I'd missed my target, and this time a rather crucial one: no guaranteed London place for me just yet. I reckoned that the unusually hot April temperatures in London had robbed me of the precious few minutes I needed to get my qualifying time, so I resolved to do an Autumn marathon to have another go: Cardiff was chosen as my target race. On the day we had some gripes about the course, as there appeared to have been some last minute changes. Our GPS devices all claimed we'd run about 27 miles rather than the standard 26.2, but the organisers were adamant it was an accurately measured course. Two of the one-mile sections around the bay took three minutes longer to run than any of the other mile splits, which I guess must have been a temporal anomaly on the accurately measured course. Despite the Einsteinian impediments I still managed a respectable 3 hours 41 minutes, so I continued to chip away at my marathon best. More importantly it meant I was guaranteed a place in the London Marathon.

Unfortunately I was too late with my qualifying time for the next spring in London, but I'd also qualified for the historic Boston marathon, and I wasn't too late for that one. My spring marathon would thus be run further afield.

Boston was incredible. The Boston Marathon is the world's oldest, having been run continuously for over 100 years. It is one of the world marathon majors, receiving global television coverage, and attracting huge crowds of spectators. Entry into Boston, unlike London, is strictly by qualifying times. Only the best runners get to do it. I was amongst the privileged.

It really did feel like a privilege to be standing at the start with all the other women. Unlike London where one is stood next to chancers in football shirts, seriously lacking in training, I felt I was in the company of some seriously talented runners. Due to their faster qualification times, most of the men were in the faster start pens further up the road, leaving me standing with mostly women. I looked around at their toned bodies and felt a sense of belonging: I deserved to be here.

The course was tough, as expected, with a series of hills culminating in Heartbreak Hill at 20 miles. The expected pain in my legs, caused by all the downhill pounding, duly arrived, but I was ready for it and battled on. The screaming crowds helped hide the severe pain from my knees and kept me going. As was now traditional for me, with a target of 3:30, I finished in 3:31, and another personal best.

A few weeks later I ran the Isle of Wight marathon, and to my delight I was an age group winner. I was getting to be something of a marathon specialist.

I'd studied the science of training and read most of the books available and now understood what worked for me and what didn't, so that I was getting more and more effective with my training. I was also passing on this knowledge to others, through a regular blog charting my progress and describing some of the training experiments I was performing on myself. I also got qualified as a level 2 UK Athletics coach, and enjoyed devising new sessions for my running club. The VO2max session I devised through my research remains one of the club's most popular to this day.

My ambitions were getting loftier and I now set my sights on our running club women's marathon record, with an Autumn marathon in Abingdon. This time my jinx of running against targets didn't hold and I broke the record by seconds in a time of 3:24. There was disappointment however when I thought I'd won a bronze medal in the National Masters Championships. The results were announced, and my time was faster than the woman in third place in my age group. I checked with the organisers and was told that entering the race wasn't sufficient: I also had to enter the championships explicitly. It was simply a matter of ticking a box on the paper entry form, but my online entry didn't appear to have that option. The organisers wouldn't reconsider. I was defeated by technology.

Even so, I'd had the best year of my running life, and it was about to get better: I'd been nominated for a sports award with my local borough. I was nominated for veteran sportswoman of the year based on my four marathons run that year, the club record, and my coaching work. I attended the local council chambers to hear about 70-year-old power lifters, junior golf champions, regional champion footballers, netball players, judoka; in fact the whole sporting spectrum seemed to be represented. It came to my category and I was mightily impressed with the achievements of my fellow nominees; the winner would be most deserving. Well they clearly thought I was the most deserving as I was called up to receive my trophy for Veteran Sportswoman of the Year. Wow!

We sat through the rest of the categories, applauding the talents of the trophy winners and runners up. Next was the keynote speech from a local professional golfer, which proved rather entertaining. I'd assumed that would be the end of the night's entertainments but there was more: there was one final category, the winner chosen from all of the category winners, that of Sports Personality of the Year. I won. Wow! I don't know whether my minor fame as a former GB international windsurfer had helped, or whether it was the writing prowess of our club chairman in singing my praises on the nomination form, but wow! I was incredibly flattered. Wow!

In all the wonderful things that had happened to me that year, I couldn't help wondering if it would have been different if people had known I was trans. The one thing I was certain of was that I deserved to compete equally: being trans did not bestow an advantage on me. Trans people, provided they are two years post-op, are now permitted to enter the Olympics: there is no advantage. As I've already mentioned, I'd say there is a disadvantage, as my power to weight ratio suffers due to my larger frame. I was in contact with other women my age through online groups, who were doing the same volume and intensity of training as me and they were getting much better results; I did find that a little frustrating, I confess, but that might just be poor genetics. So no advantage for me, but I wonder how my clubmates would feel if they knew a trans woman held the club women's marathon record? Maybe one day I will find out.

I got great satisfaction from entering women-only races. One of the first races I ever did was the *Race For Life* series of events: these are women-only races in aid of breast cancer. As a woman, it's such a relaxed and happy event in the absence of men: you don't feel the eyes of everyone on you as you stand semi-undressed on the start line. Many men I've spoken to just don't seem to get it: they complain about the exclusion of men from these events. They don't seem to understand that a mixed race would be just the same as any other, with a predominantly male field, and women discouraged from entering. They don't understand what it's like feeling you are being judged for how you look. They don't need to worry about depilating and waxing or whether a pair of shorts or trousers creates too much of a muffin top or camel toe.

As a trans woman I felt an extra dimension to women only races: it was like a rite of passage. It felt like the ultimate confirmation of my gender: I stood among my equals, my sisters. Ultimately though they're just a really good laugh, without any men to push you out of the way.

I was a regular at one women's race in particular: a long-standing 5-mile race through beautiful country lanes. Unlike the Race For Life, which was a fun event where times were not recorded, this race was a far more serious affair: it attracted some really good runners hoping to win some money. This was the one race where I was justified in standing with my toe right on the start line. Usually in races you stand a distance back from the line according to your pace, with the slowest at the back; this is just common sense really as you can't all start on the line. I once ran into the back of someone walking at the 1-mile mark in the Great South Run; to be that far ahead and walking, they must have started right on the start line. I wonder how many people had collided with them? That's just selfish.

I've had a good record at that women's 5-miler, usually placing well or winning my age category. The best I ever did overall was fifth place. Unfortunately I have to leave the youngsters to battle it out for the win; my chance for overall glory has slipped away with the sands of time. Or so I thought.

Despite my success in London, the greatest race of my life was my local 5-mile trail race. It's not very often I get to run it, as I'm one of the organisers, but one year I thought I'd give it a blast. As luck would have it, the local superstar girl, our Olympic hopeful, didn't turn up. It's always a bit depressing to stand next to a talented athlete and know that even if she just had a gentle-paced training run, there's no way you could get anywhere near her. She was a friend, and I had the deepest respect and admiration for her, but I was so glad she hadn't turned up. Instead I had Emma and Sam to contend with. I knew I could beat Emma on a good day, but despite getting close to Sam, I'd never yet beaten her. I was in good form though so reckoned this could be a good battle.

We are lined up a few rows back from the start, with the fast men ahead of us. I'm next to Sam and Emma with a few other girls around us. I don't recognise some of the others, but as they are from local clubs I figure I'd have known them if they were fast. I'm relaxed and ready. The gun goes and we are off down the trail. Sam goes off at quite a pace, which even for her seems a little quick; I know my pace well and hang back and try not to panic; if I went off with Sam I'd blow up after only a couple of miles. We settle down into our running and I'm about sixth place amongst the women, as Sam drags the others along with her. My judgement of the other's ability proves accurate as one by one they drop away, having gone off too quickly with Sam. After two miles I'm in third behind Emma and Sam, and closing steadily on Emma.

Just before the half way point I catch Emma, and as I pass one of my friends marshalling, he shouts "You're second. You're catching her". I can now see Sam in the distance. I'm trying to gauge how quickly I'm closing: there's less than two miles now and she's still a fair way ahead. I feel good, having conserved my energy early on, and I try to up my pace just a little. We are now at one mile to go and Sam is much closer: she is definitely catchable, but how much has she left in the tank? With half a mile to go I'm only a few strides behind her and start to consider tactics: do I wait and try to out-sprint her, or do I pass now and try to break her in the remaining half mile? I remember the advice I've read: when you pass, do so decisively so that the person can't stay with you - you need to break the elastic connecting the two of you.

This is my moment. I move up a gear and charge past Sam. I have to keep this pace going. I can feel my heart pounding, my lungs bursting and the lactate burning in my legs. *Keep going. Keep going. Don't look back.* I remind myself I only have a couple of minutes more running to endure. *400 metres. Keep going.* Soon I can see the finish line. I have no idea where Sam is, but fear her sprint finish. *You want this. You want this badly. Give it everything you have.* I pick up the pace again, trying to block out the pain, and as I near the finish line I give it one final sprint. I cross the line completely spent, and as I come to a standstill I grey out and my knees buckle. I'm helped through the finish line funnel by my friends all cheering. I've won my first ever race.

I suspect that's the only chance I'll ever get to win a race; I'm now over fifty and I suspect will have to be content with contesting my age group. To be honest, I was lucky with who turned up at the race: there are no end of talented local women who would easily beat me. They didn't turn up though, and I won. That was a tick in the box; an ambition achieved.

There was one further ambition I had yet to achieve in the running world. My marathon best was now at 3:22; if I could just knock another 7 minutes off it, then I would qualify for the elite start of the London Marathon. I'd always envied the group of talented women on the separate earlier women's elite start. On the front would be the main contenders such as Paula

Radcliffe, but behind, and often cheekily waving at the camera, would be the talented club runners who'd run the qualifying time of 3:15. I wanted to be one of those runners.

I could have chosen any marathon to set my 3:15 qualifying time, but I chose the country's most crowded: the London Marathon. Training had been going well, and I knew I was capable of hitting my target, but things didn't get off to the best of starts. I was on the *Good For Age* start line along with the cream of the nation's club runners. This would seem like the perfect recipe for a quick getaway except for a major flaw: positioned ahead of us on the start line were 'celebrities'. I've often wondered what purpose 'celebrities' serve in road races; no doubt they raise the profile for their charities and give some extra interest for TV viewers, but what do they actually bring to the race itself? Why do 'celebrities' deserve to be placed on the *Good For Age* start line ahead of a thousand of the country's best runners, who almost by definition will be faster than any of the 'celebrities'?

The start was carnage. As the gun went, it was a mad scramble to try get past the slower 'celebrities'. The particular problem that year was the presence of the Maasai warriors: with their spears and shields they made the perfect road block. I had a date with destiny, but instead I was walking behind a load of guys in full ceremonial dress looking like they were trying to chase a small mammal out of the undergrowth. My only option seemed to be to get onto the pavement and run behind the line of spectators at the roadside; a few "excuse me"s and "sorry"s later and I was back on course ahead of the road warriors. I'd lost 3 minutes to the battle.

There was no point in trying to rush to make up lost time as I knew I'd pay for it later. I knew what effort I was capable of, so kept pushing at that pace, knowing that I would still get in under 3:15, but a little closer than anticipated.

After a few miles I realised I'd been running next to the same woman for some time.
"3:15?"
"Yes"
"I'm Anne"
"Annie"

"I won't chat"
"Thanks"
"But can we pace?"
"Great"
My new friend and I stayed together for the next 17 miles. At drinks stations we shared water; we shared the pacing; we shared very few words. There was a bond though, through our common purpose.

We were on target and running comfortably, but as we entered the difficult final stages the course suddenly got crowded as the road went slightly uphill. I tried to maintain even effort, fearful of going into oxygen debt working against the incline. Annie though maybe had a little spare capacity and maintained an even pace up the rise. I lost her.

This will always be one of the great imponderables: what would have happened if I'd stuck with Annie? The moment I was on my own I started to struggle. At first my pace was only a few seconds per mile down, but as the finish line got closer my pace started to really suffer. As we entered the City of London I felt like I was already a spent force but there were still 4 miles to go. My neck had gone, and the only comfortable position was to run with my head thrown back. In the photos I looked like I was gasping for air with my head back, although I guess I was to some extent.

I was now looking at my watch with each mile marker: at my current pace I was still a minute inside the target. All I had to do was maintain my current pace and I'd achieve my greatest running ambition. It was hot though. The sun was beating down in clear blue skies and my head was beginning to throb with the exertion and pain.

Another mile down but my pace had dropped some more. This was going to be really close.

I was now playing mind games with myself.
*There's only another 20 minutes of running. Keep pushing!*
*But it hurts!*
*Of course it hurts. This is the test! Don't give in.*
*But it's not worth it.*
*Of course it's worth it. You've worked all year for this.*
*But I can't give any more.*
*Yes you can. You have to.*

*But we're on target. There's no need to push any harder.*
*You have to give everything or you'll regret it. Push.* **Push. PUSH!**

And so it went on.
**Push! Push!**
As we entered the last mile I still felt I could make it, but knew it was going to be close. We rounded the last corner at Buckingham Palace and I tried to sprint for all I was worth, but nothing came: my pace remained unchanged. Even with the sight of the finish line I couldn't elicit any more effort. I was completely spent. There was nothing left in the tank.

The clock read 3:14, but I knew I had a minute in hand as we had timing chips on our shoes and it had taken me a minute to cross the timing mat at the start. I had 90 seconds to sprint The Mall to the finish line. The clock hit 3:15 and though I knew I had to give everything, I really couldn't: I was exhausted. It's difficult in that state to keep all the numbers in your head but as the clock hit 3:16 I knew it was all over. I crossed the line only a few seconds later, but I'd failed: I'd missed 3:15 by only a few seconds.

I managed a smile for my finish line photo and medal pose, but I felt sick: both literally and mentally. I felt hollow: again both the nausea of having spent every last drop of energy, and the emptiness of ambitions denied. My reward bar of chocolate in my kit bag just stuck in my mouth: it seemed bitter and tasteless. Where was my reward?

I managed to get some bottles of sport drink down me, and as my dehydration waned and my energy levels improved I contented myself with the fact that I might be allowed an elite place anyway having only missed qualification by mere seconds. The London Marathon organisers had other ideas though: conditions had been favourable and they had no shortage of qualifying times. My ambitions were not to be fulfilled.

I had smashed my own PB though, together with my own club record. I am proud to say I ran the London Marathon in 3 hours 15 minutes. What might have been though?

Annie did brilliantly, and from the point I lost her she just got faster, finishing in 3:12. She ran the second half faster than the first half, which takes exceptional talent.

The great unanswerable question: am I the fastest trans woman to ever run the London Marathon? Such is the nature of stealth living, I guess we'll never know!

# Coming out, part 2

I live in what we call stealth: hardly anyone outside my family knows my trans history. Stealth is a term I'm not completely comfortable with, because it implies some form of subterfuge. I'm not living a lie; I'm living the truth. You'd imagine that my truth gives me great satisfaction, and to a large extent it does. You'd also imagine that a fully stealth existence is what most trans people want, and to a large extent it is. I am a woman first and foremost, and that is my truth; that is how I live my life. I am also a trans woman, and am proud of all the problems I've overcome to get to this point in my life. Not being able to share those experiences can feel quite isolating. Sometimes stealth doesn't feel quite like the ideal lifestyle it first seemed.

Whenever I get close to someone I always end up in a debate with myself about whether to disclose my trans history. With potential romantic partners then I believe there is a duty to disclose; I don't believe you can have an intimate relationship and be concealing a whole part of you from your partner. Some trans people don't disclose, and that is their decision alone, but I don't think you can really open your soul to someone without sharing all of your experiences.

With close platonic relationships, the issue of disclosure is less clear cut. I have a lot of close friends who know nothing of my trans history, and there is no immediate need to disclose, but just as with romantic relationships, it feels like there isn't such a close bond when they don't know of my past.

In the early nineties, with Dougie gone, and with me yet to re-establish contact with my Aunt's side of the family, I suddenly found myself in a position where no one I was in regular contact with knew of my past: I'd lost touch with my friends from my previous job, and suddenly I was, for the first time ever, 100% stealth. It felt incredibly isolating. It was a bad time for me anyway having found the break up with Dougie very hard to take, and I was suffering badly from depression. I resolved to have therapy, through the company's employee assistance program.

I was put in contact with a therapist called Beth, who worked out of her house in a small village fifteen miles away. It was my first appointment and there I was sitting face to face with her in Liberty-print upholstered bamboo chairs, with her asking me to talk about my problems. Why did I not just state straight-out that I was trans? For thirty minutes I talked about my alienation from my family, my split with Dougie, and my profound sense of loneliness, but I struggled to explain the primary cause of these events. I seemed to have no problem telling disrespectful doctors that I am trans, and yet I struggled to explain this to someone for whom it was crucial they know.

Eventually, during that first session, I was able to come out to my therapist, who of course acted like it was just another piece of my history I was discussing, and no big deal. This is of course exactly as it should have been, particularly for someone with her training. For me though, the dam burst, almost literally: I was in floods of tears. I was cataloging all the hurt I'd suffered at the hands of my family, telling her all the personal things I'd kept locked away for years, and hadn't even been able to discuss with Dougie. At the end of the session I was a wreck, and had to return to work feeling numb and shaky.

Our therapy sessions continued for many weeks until I was able to talk about anything in my past without breaking down. My next coming out would be somewhat easier I imagined, and I didn't have to wait very long to put that to the test.

I'd fallen for Simon, one of my colleagues. He was the perfect man: a physics PhD, a fitness fanatic with an amazing physique, gorgeous looking, witty, well paid; he had not one negative point. I knew he had feelings for me too, especially after some playful fumblings on a weekend away with our friends. I didn't want a repeat of the problems with Dougie, disclosing a long way into our relationship, so on our drive back from the weekend retreat I decided to tell all. I was a little emotional telling my story, but I remained calm and there were no tears this time. Simon seemed to take it really well and seemed absolutely fine. I didn't tell him my true feelings for him, thinking that could wait until we next saw each other.

Simon had to work away and I didn't see him for a while. The next time I saw him was at the office Christmas party: he turned up with my friend Shona, who was showing off the engagement ring he'd bought her. I was devastated. I managed to hold it together to attend their wedding, but I kept thinking that if I wasn't trans then that could have been me walking down the aisle. I would have looked so much better than Shona: she really didn't do that dress justice.

My best friend Jacqui had to put up with my "it could have been me" rants about the wedding. We were close and shared most things, but she didn't know I was trans. Eventually I got over my heartbreak with Simon and got back onto an even keel and back into the party vibe. One evening we were getting ready for a party, and I was getting changed round at her place. We were in her bedroom, and she stripped off in front of me to put on her dress. She thought nothing of this, but my reaction surprised me somewhat: I couldn't take my eyes off her. I'd never felt like this before. I'd only ever had relationships with men and had always thought I was straight. One girl crush doesn't necessarily make me gay, but it raised many questions in me, and unsettled me a little: back then I thought gender identity and sexuality were related, something I now know not to be the case, and realising I might not be entirely straight seemed somehow to be a betrayal of everything I'd been through.

Whatever my conclusions about my sexuality, these feelings seemed to mark a turning point in our relationship and I decided it was time to come out to her. I didn't really believe that a sexual relationship was a possibility, although I had wondered, but the extra level of intimacy meant that in my mind some sort of coming-out threshold had been passed.

Coming out seemed remarkably straightforward: I guess Jacqui was a little surprised but she took it all in her stride. I amazed myself at how calm and relaxed I was: I was starting to get the hang of this. She had all the usual questions about when I transitioned, how old I was when I first knew, and what it was like at school. Jacqui had already known I had a troubled past with my parents and brother and so it was a relief for her to finally understand what had gone on; she had always wondered just why arguments with my father had led to such an irretrievable breakdown.

Our friendship from that point reached new heights, with girly activities undertaken together such as beauty treatments and shopping trips. There were problems though. I started to think that maybe she viewed me as something of a project. She now realised that I'd never been coached in the art of being a girl, for instance no one had ever told me that the way to avoid a lipstick mark on a glass is to lick the rim of the glass before taking a sip. I'd get makeup advice and be told about the latest must-have tinted moisturiser: all useful stuff. She persuaded me to bleach my hair and cut it short: great fashion idea, but not so practical if you are concerned about looking masculine emerging from the water in a wetsuit. I started to feel like she had taken on the role of mother.

I could have tolerated her mothering of me, but our relationship was under greater strain in the opposite direction: a strain that would eventually break us apart. I suddenly had someone in my life who knew my trans history and so I could share all the things with her that I couldn't share with anyone else; there was a lot I wanted to share. Professional therapy had ended for me, but I entered into a form of therapy in my moments alone with Jacqui. I would unburden myself of all the things that had bothered me over the years. Jacqui was very patient with me and would always listen, and to me she seemed a total angel. Then two terrible events conspired against us.

Jacqui had a very close friend called Charlotte: they were like sisters. Charlotte had gone on holiday with her boyfriend to Thailand. While out swimming, the two of them had got into trouble in a strong current and been swept out to sea. Charlotte's boyfriend had made it back and raised the alarm, but tragically Charlotte was never found. Jacqui was devastated, unsurprisingly, and turned to me for support.

At the same time as Jacqui received her news, I received my own terrible news: my mum was dying of cancer. That news would have been bad enough as it was, but my family situation made it a whole lot worse: my father was refusing to let me see her. After all our years apart my mum was still letting my father rule her. Looking back, I should have ignored him and visited her, but I was still emotionally fragile when it came to dealing with them and I obeyed his instructions to stay away. It weighed heavily on me, but I never told Jacqui.

Around the time of my fortieth birthday, my relationship with Jacqui seemed to get strained and we saw less and less of each other. Eventually we drifted apart, she moved, and I never saw her again. I was always puzzled over what came between us, until a few years ago I found out after a chance online meeting with Jacqui. She said I was self obsessed: I only ever talked about myself and the problems of being trans. Just when she needed me to be there for her I let her down. She said that the final straw came on my fortieth birthday: she thought I would have had a big party, which was just the tonic she needed, but instead I just moped around depressed and couldn't be bothered to even go out for drinks. She couldn't believe I could be so selfish.

I was shocked by her outburst, but it rang true: I could see how selfish I appeared. I had no idea how talking through my problems with her had affected her and our relationship. I must admit I'd underestimated the effect Charlotte's death had had on her. I never told her about my mum's cancer.

Shortly after my fortieth birthday my mum died. I never got to see her, and she never got to see female me. She took to her grave some fantasy notion of a son she never had. She never met her daughter. My father kept his pledge of never allowing me back into his life and banned me from her funeral: like a fool, I obeyed.

One of the practical issues of non-disclosure with female friends is when chat turns to particularly female aspects of the human condition. I guess my friends have always sensed a certain reluctance on my part to talk about my monthly cycle, and mercifully not pressed too much on the subject. Once I hit my late forties though, I did confess to one friend that I was on hormone replacement therapy, HRT.

I'd opened the floodgates. I had identified myself as menopausal to someone who was herself menopausal. We now had common ground for intimate discussions of all things menstrual, or so she thought; it made for some very awkward discussions. Fortunately I had experienced menopause symptoms when I'd come off HRT for facial surgery some years earlier, so I could at least relate to the symptoms she was experiencing. What do you tell someone though, when she asks when are you going to come off HRT? I didn't think I could answer "never?".

My most uncomfortable conversation was when she learnt I had an appointment with a gynaecologist. It was after I'd purchased a set of dilators: I wasn't making any progress in terms of accommodating the largest dilator and I'd made myself very sore. I needed time off for the appointment and I let it slip it was gynaecological. She wanted to know what I was seeing the gynaecologist for and all I could think to tell her was about my old problems of pain during sexual intercourse. This then let her open up about her similar issues, and when it all got rather awkward I wondered if I should just come out to her right there in the meeting room at work, but I held my ground. I had her sympathy though, as it seemed to her I was going through exactly what she had been through. After some searching questions, and me giving vague answers and blushing, she let it drop.

I got very close to coming out that day, but I left that heart-to-heart with a little humour to help me on my way. Her closing remark:
"Who the hell would want to be a woman?"

# Can I help you sir?

**sir** (sə:)
noun
Used as a polite or respectful way of addressing a man, especially one in a position of authority:
*Excuse me, sir.*

**sir²** (sə:)
verb [with object]
To misgender a woman by use of the word sir:
*Excuse me, sir.*

**sirred** (sə:d)
Past tense of **sir**:
*I was sirred again today.*

To a trans woman, *sir* is such a hurtful word. We so desperately want to be accepted by society as our true gender, that the merest hint of *sir* in a conversation can ruin an otherwise pleasant day. We are fragile souls, and to be addressed as *sir* can be a crushing blow. After being sirred, it could take me two days to feel fully on top of things again. The further I got into transition and the longer between occurrences of sirring, the bigger the blow seemed to be. Just as I felt I'd fully assimilated into society as a woman, a misplaced *sir* could bring that all crashing down.

I'd often wonder just what it was that caused a sirring. It most often happened on the phone, and there's an obvious explanation for that, but the face to face sirrings often had me mystified. I'm wearing a dress and makeup, and a guy looks up from his desk and says "Can I help you sir?". To be fair, my look of shock at being addressed thus would often result in "Oh I'm terribly sorry madam", but there were occasions when the guy, and it was usually a man, would stand his ground and not correct himself. Why?

Studies have shown that identifying someone as female is more about the absence of male gender cues than the presence of female cues[26]. It's suggested that it only takes one male gender cue to override as many as four female gender cues, such is the male dominated world we live in. Thus we might have long hair, makeup, dress, and boobs, but a deep voice could still shout *man* at some people. It seems to me that there are intellectual overrides happening: a reasoning person who picks up a male gender cue in an otherwise female-presenting person would know to address that person as female. My experience has shown that children and the intellectually challenged don't have that social judgement and the small male cues trump all the female ones: I will remind you once more of my friend's husband who mumbled "Nancy boy" whenever I was near.

I can forgive some people for sirring me; prior to my facial surgery, if I was a dishevelled mess in androgynous clothing at the end of a workout then I may well have confused some people. However, I have been sirred when presenting clearly as female, and I take this as blatant trans-misogyny on the part of the sirrer. If someone is presented with sufficient gender cues to indicate that a person is identifying as female, then to sir them is to take away a person's right to self determination, which is the ultimate form of disrespect.

I am a stereotype; I admit it. Over the years I've tried to remove any male gender cues, to try to avoid the dreaded *sir*. I try not to overcompensate in my style of dress, but I like to leave no doubt as to my gender. After earlier experiments with short hair, I now keep my hair long, in a female style. I wear makeup to go out, but I keep it understated. My height is a concern but 5'10" isn't so unusual.

There is now just one aspect of me which I think sometimes lets me down: my voice.

---

[26] Suzanne J. Kessler and Wendy McKenna - Gender: An Ethnomethodological Approach

# Speech therapy

The voice: the one thing every trans woman worries about. I say *every* trans woman, but there are some youngsters who were lucky enough to receive testosterone blockers before puberty and so their voice never broke: you are very lucky girls and I wish you all the best. For the rest of us older generation, and the younger generation who aren't fortunate to have the parental support and funds for pre-puberty blockers, testosterone has damaged us and broken our voices.

Testosterone is something of a super-hormone: unlike the meek polite œstrogen, it struts around in its leathers and cape wreaking havoc on the young body. In some, maybe most, the changes it leaves in its wake are welcome; for others, generally trans women, it's a cause of heartache. Testosterone is the trans woman's poison.

The damage that testosterone does to a trans woman's body is largely irreversible. Some changes it brings, such as body hair, muscle and skin tone, do recover somewhat once the supply of testosterone is cut off; other changes such as facial hair and bone structure require some form of intervention. While facial features can be feminised to quite a striking degree, some faces will always look to some small degree masculine. Some areas of the body are currently beyond surgical intervention: many of us trans women will always be tall, have larger than average feet, and larger than average hands.

I guess I'm fortunate in many respects, as skeletally I fall within reasonably female bounds on the size spectrum, albeit at the tall end. The one area that has always bothered me though is my voice. When I transitioned there were no surgical procedures to raise a deep voice. Nowadays there are some procedures available for feminising the voice but they are risky and not suitable for everyone. Just as the effects of testosterone hadn't been too drastic on the rest of my body, my voice wasn't too deep, but it was nevertheless a male voice.

I tried to speak at the top end of my range, but to me it sounded artificial and weak. I felt that, even if I appeared presentably female, as soon as I opened my mouth I was announcing to the world I was trans. If I could meet someone in person then I would usually be addressed as *madam*, but on the phone I was invariably addressed as *sir*.

I was most relieved then, when the folks at Charing Cross Hospital sent me for speech therapy. I imagined this to be the end of my problems: gone would be my awful man-voice, to be replaced by something more appropriate to my appearance. I was under no illusions I would be able to manage some high-pitched little-girl voice, but I was hoping for at least something at the lower end of the range you'd expect for a 5'10" woman.

My speech therapy session was a total disappointment. It went something like this:
"Well you have nothing to worry about. Your voice sounds fine. Just remember to try to keep your voice in the upper part of your range."

If my voice sounded so fine, then why did everyone always call me sir on the telephone?

For years I hated using the telephone, and would go out of my way to avoid using one. I'd always try to speak to someone face to face in preference to a quick call. Doctors' appointments would be made by visiting the surgery rather than making a phone call. I almost missed the date of my vaginoplasty because the hospital had expected me to phone in, but I'd delayed and delayed, frightened of using a simple device that most of us take for granted.

I was fragile in my early years after transition. My confidence would increase with each passing day, until I'd get misgendered, usually by being called *sir* on the phone. My ego would come crashing down and I'd be in a rut for days, beginning the cycle of slowly picking myself up all over again. It was so critical to my own sense of identity that the entire world see me as female, that even an anonymous nobody on the other end of the phone could put me in a tail spin.

My confidence was at its highest when in the company of friends: everybody knew I was female regardless of how deep my voice was, and I had no fear of being misgendered. Things were very different in the company of strangers though.

I'd been invited to a friend's birthday party. There would be a handful of people I knew, our mutual friends, but the majority of the people would be strangers. I wasn't completely relaxed, nervous about how I would be perceived. It helped that for the Roman-themed party I was wearing a very pretty goddess-style dress, wearing my femininity with pride. I was still nervous about my voice though, and without really thinking about it I cranked the pitch up an extra notch.

A mutual friend came over and joined in the chat I was having with some strangers. In front of the group she said to me "You sound really odd. What's up?".

I was quite shocked. I made an excuse about my throat being dry, and went off to find wine. I took a step back from myself and realised that I'd been talking so far up my range that I'd lost all variation in pitch, and was talking in a strange whiny monotone. I was so embarrassed to realise how I must have sounded.

In those pre-Internet days I had no YouTube videos to coach me on how to speak, so I had to figure it out myself. I'd heard of singers talking about head voice and chest voice, and that seemed to make some sense to me in terms of my pitch: when I speak I can feel the height of my voice. When I'm pitching high, it's as if I can locate the source of my voice as somewhere inside my head. As I lower my voice, I feel the location getting lower down into my throat and down to the voice box. As I continue to lower my voice it passes the voice box and descends into my chest. I've not researched this to know if there is an actual physical effect going on, but that description seems real to me. On that basis, I guess I always keep my voice above the level of my voice box.

I also realised that modulation was important, and this was something that came far more natural to me. As my transition progressed I became more at peace with myself and happier in my skin. With this new sense of self came the blossoming of my true personality and my speech became more animated: more feminine. Speaking in a monotone is a very male pattern, and is something I feel I'm still guilty of when I get a bit depressed or tired. A bubbly me though, is a feminine me.

Still the doubts about my voice remained: if the person I was addressing couldn't see me then I was still nervous about my voice, which itself had a detrimental effect, slipping back into monotone. I was always nervous about meeting people for the first time on the telephone, something that was happening increasingly often with the conference calls I was attending at work.

The telephone nerves were nothing though compared to my encounters with blind people. The first thing a blind person experiences on meeting me, and often the only thing, is my voice. That may be supplemented with a shake of my larger than average hand. My voice will be issuing from a point a few inches higher than your average female. I don't feel I'm representing myself with my most feminine qualities. I always dread to imagine the mental imagine the blind person has of me.

I recently had a video call with a young blind trans woman; she knew I was trans but I was still nervous. The call started humorously with the screen completely black and I realised she was in total darkness: why would a blind woman ever need to put a light on? We managed to get some light, and the camera pointed in the right direction ("Up a little, to the right, sorry, your left, too far, that's it!"), and had a fine old chat. It took me a while to relax, as I was very conscious of my voice, but after a few minutes I was back to my natural self. At the end of the call she commented that I didn't have the highest of voices, but I sounded completely female, and that she wished she sounded like me. I was flattered and relieved.

I haven't been sirred on calls for some time now. I'm sure this is mostly down to me feeling more relaxed with the technology. Alexander Graham Bell invented the telephone one hundred and thirty seven years ago, and it's taken me twenty eight years to master the use of it.

# Coming out, part 3

*1984*

This chapter is part three in the coming out saga, but chronologically it's the first. I left the most difficult chapter 'til last: how do you tell your mother that her worst nightmares have come true? How do you explain that her son, despite all outward appearances and common sense, is actually her daughter? How do you explain that the stories she's read in the *News of the World*, of men in dresses, of freaks and weirdos, are about to be enacted before her?

I'm pretty sure you don't do it the way I did.

Let me make one thing clear, in case you haven't got the message yet: I'm not a freak, weirdo, or a man, but the press do like to portray us in a very biased way. I would always make sure my parents saw the Sunday newspaper stories of trans people and try to gauge their reaction: it was never good.
"It's disgusting how they carry on."
"He still looks like a man."
"They're just doing it for attention."
"Isn't she the one who's, you know, a bit funny?"
I think that last remark was the best of a bad bunch: my mum thought Caroline Cossey, the model Tula, was "a bit funny", funny peculiar, not funny ha-ha.

Talk of anything away from the straight and narrow was taboo in our house. My parents had been too embarrassed to have that one talk parents are supposed to have with their sexually awakening children; I honestly couldn't ever imagine them broaching the subject with me. I deliberately baited my mum once:
"Mum, what's sex?"
She went bright red and was completely silent, frozen to the spot like a startled rabbit, unable to put any form of reply together. I let her squirm just long enough before letting her off the hook:
"It's what posh people have their coal delivered in."

The look of relief on her face was a joy to behold.

My relationship with my father had deteriorated beyond the point of no return. We argued about everything; he had to rule me totally, unable to let me have my way in anything. The days of being punished for gender-role infringements were long gone, I was too careful in my behaviour now, but every conversation we had seemed to end in an argument. I truly hated my father: he seemed so mean-spirited and hateful. I despised him for his racism: he ran a grocer's shop in the heart of what had become the Asian district of Wolverhampton and his blatant racism was driving customers away. When the Liverpool Toxteth race riots spilled over into Wolverhampton, his shop was ransacked and the words *Racist Bastard* painted on the wall. We stood amongst the wreckage of the shop, with him close to tears and exclaiming "How can they accuse me of that?", to which I replied:
"Because you are a racist". I never came home from university again after that; that's not a statement you can recover from.

It was against this background that I started my Gender Identity Clinic treatment, hiding in London, afraid to return home. I was now on hormones and still hadn't told my parents. I knew I was going to have to tell them but I'd left it all rather late. With hindsight I know I should have visited them and told them face to face, but I was scared of a possibly violent reaction. I chose the telephone as my medium of disclosure.

"Mum, I'm transsexual. I'm going to have a sex change. I'm going to become a woman."

Those aren't words that the average mother would ever want to hear, but I hoped she'd at least try to understand the pain I'd lived with all my life. I expected the words to at least open up a dialogue between us so that I could explain what I'd been through. There were all the incidents of my childhood which, after swift corrective action, had never been spoken of. Now all the jigsaw pieces must surely fall into place for her, as I was able to explain my behavioural idiosyncrasies.

Her reaction was beyond anything I could ever have imagined.

Her scream was as if someone had run her through with a sword. I waited and waited, and eventually through the sobbing could hear a shaky voice saying "No...no...no...". I couldn't talk to her. I wanted to expand on my initial rather stark statement, but couldn't get through to her. All I was getting was "How could you do this to us?...How could you do this to us?". Eventually I told her I'd phone back later.

It occurs to me now as I write this, that there seemed a total acceptance of the truth of what I was saying. They later claimed that this was a bolt from the blue, but if that was the case, then surely the more likely reaction would have been one of incredulity: maybe a claim that this was some sort of a joke. It seems to me that I was telling her something that she'd hoped all my life was never going to happen; she insisted that wasn't the case.

My next phone call was just as traumatic, but this time it was me in tears. In twenty four hours she'd gone from breakdown to complete and utter denial. It was like talking to a brick wall: I couldn't get through to her at all. She wouldn't accept any explanation from me, but just kept telling me how I'd been led astray living in London and that I must come home immediately and stop all this nonsense. At the most vulnerable time in my life I felt completely alone trying to talk to my mother. At the end of the call I was sobbing uncontrollably, feeling completely abandoned.

The calls were all happening within earshot of my friend Andrea, who'd rented me a room. By the end of the third call I was such an emotional wreck that my legs had gone and I was slumped on the floor begging my mum to listen to me. Andrea grabbed the phone off me, said a few choice words to my mum, and hung up. Now Andrea was getting blamed for talking me into all this nonsense.

In all the conversations with my mum, it was always what I was doing to *her;* it was the disgrace I was bringing on the family; it was what everyone else was telling me to do; at no point did she ever try to understand what I was feeling. After many phone calls the brick wall had not even the slightest crack in it. I decided to move away, get my own flat, and begin the process of transition on my own.

My new flat was euphemistically called 'The Garden Flat': it was the rear room of a large house that had been turned into six flats. I accessed the flat through the flimsy patio door, through the garden at the rear. It had a tiny kitchen partitioned off from the room, and a tinier shower room that had been squeezed in under the stairs in my small bit of partitioned off hallway. I was aware there was no phone when I moved in, but this felt empowering as it was now up to me to walk to the phone box to make a call, rather than suffer being phoned up at all hours just to be shouted at.

My father had been absent in all the shouting. The one time he'd actually answered the phone, he immediately handed over to my mum, with a dismissive "It's for you". I wonder if he'd meant anything by the word "it"? Now that I was living in isolation and limiting my calls to them, he finally sprung into action. However in doing so he ably demonstrated what an utter coward he was, completely unable to deal with me: he sent his brothers-in-law down to London to sort me out.

I'd reached the stage in my transition where I was living part-time in girl mode but most of the time in boy mode as I hadn't yet come out at work. I came home one day in boy mode to find three of my uncles waiting for me on my patio-doorstep. They'd had great trouble finding 'The Garden Flat' but here they were. I knew this wasn't going to be a friendly visit, in fact I was terrified. Why had my monster of a father sent three heavies down for me? More to the point, why did he not have the courage to deal with the problem himself, and send three people in his place? I wondered whether I was going to be bound and gagged and thrown in the back of a van. There was no van. Good.

I got the same lecture I'd had on the phone, but at least this time there was interaction. Maybe they could see the pain on my face, or the sincerity with which I described my struggles, but I think I won them over. Is this how it might have gone if I'd come out face to face with my mum? The fact that my mum never let me back into her life perhaps says I was always going to lose, but I think things might have been different in the absence of my father.

My father *was* absent though, and maybe that was for the best. His cowardly way of not dealing with my situation and sending his brothers-in-law maybe made things easier for me. I sent them away apparently satisfied that there was no way they could dissuade me from my chosen path. After an exhausting but mercifully short discussion they went away to report back to my parents.

After their report, you'd perhaps imagine that my parents might be concerned at my emotional state and the trauma of what I was about to go through on my own in London. No. My mum was fixated on the fact that on the floor under the chair were my shoes: not ridiculous drag-queen-style shoes, but modest one-inch-heel comfortable everyday court shoes. To her this seemed to confirm all her darkest fears. She'd seen me wearing her shoes when I was little; what did she expect? I think my mum was in denial as, according to letters she wrote to the doctors at Charing Cross Hospital, she had observed behaviours in me which were cause for suspicion. Walking around in her dress and high heels saying "Look mummy I'm pretty just like you!" is I believe a fairly clear sign!

My father's reaction was rather more pragmatic: he informed me that he'd made a will expressly to write me out of it. He also vowed never to mention me again; according to the rest of my family he made good on that promise. I recently got to see his will: he'd left small amounts of money to a lot of my extended family, and the bulk to my two nephews, who I'm informed do not know I exist. True to his word, there is no mention of me anywhere in his will.

After my uncles' 'kidnap squad' visit, I no longer felt safe. I wondered what would happen next, with my father coordinating things from his mountain lair. I was unaware at the time that Charing Cross were advising my parents to drop contact with me and let me transition in peace. I beat them to it though, with the only option I felt I had: I moved house, and didn't tell anyone where I'd moved to. I would be isolated from my family for the next nine years, before I was re-united with my wonderful aunt, uncle and cousins.

My parents never got to see gorgeous confident successful female me. I'd always assumed that my morbidly-obese chain-smoking father would die a painful death long before my mum, and that she and I would be at last united as mother and daughter. Instead, he lost weight, gave up smoking, and survived my mum by ten years. Neither he nor my mum ever got to see female me.

Would it have been different if I'd come out face to face, and maybe in girl mode? I will never know. We hear of people getting dumped by text, and are rightly shocked at the cowardice. I think I did the coming-out equivalent of dumping by text.

# A letter to my nephews

I really struggled with the decision to include this chapter: this is so deeply personal.

I'm sterile. There was never any question over whether I should carry through my plans. I'm a trans woman, ergo, I cannot have children. I never had a relationship with a woman, nor the desire for a relationship, and so the question of parenting never arose. I assume I am an XY karyotype, but my chromosomes were never tested, and neither was my fertility. The thought of being a father though horrified me: to me it would be the ultimate definition of manhood. I was female, and to me that meant I was sterile at birth: I could not carry a child.

Can a woman be a father? Yes. I now realise I was wrong. Biology does not define us. There are children out there with two women as parents: this is how the natural variation of nature works. One woman is the mother, one woman is the father. Indeed there are children of two men: one man is the mother, the other the father. Nature dictates there will always be a mother and a father, at least with the current limitations of reproductive medicine. Nature's, some might say cruel, trick is that the gender identities of the parents may not follow their reproductive biology: women can be fathers, men can be mothers.

I would have to be satisfied with vicarious parenting through my brother and his sons, but there is a problem: he always claimed to be an only child and his sons do not supposedly know I exist. I think they must have an idea about me, but my brother claims they do not.

It's always been a source of great sadness for me that I have no access to the closest I have to my own children. It causes me social problems too: I had considered not telling anyone I had a brother, but I've never been able to lie, and so admit his existence, but confess to friends I have 'very little' contact with him. 'Very little' is overplaying it somewhat, but it is the truth as I have had email contact. I have admitted to people that I have nephews, but fortunately I've managed to avoid the toughest questions and so have never had to explain why I had never met them until recently at my father's funeral. It can feel very isolating living a life of stealth.

So, after much internal debate, here is the chapter that was almost deleted: a letter, written but never sent, to my nephews.

Dear Harry and Robert,

You don't know me, but you once met me at your Grandfather's funeral. I'm the tall blonde lady in the black dress and grey cardigan. Robert, you offered me a cup of tea at the wake.

I'm your aunt, your father's sister.

I apologise if this comes as something of a shock. I'm hoping this isn't something you didn't already know about, but according to your father you don't know I exist. I know you are both intelligent boys, and may have pieced the facts together and worked it out for yourselves. I also think your mother may have told you about me, as she's been trying to get me and your father together for a long time.

You'll be wondering why your father has kept me secret all these years. I'm a trans woman. Your father is ashamed of me. He knew me as his brother, but now I am his sister. He apparently can't deal with that, and despite my attempts over the years to re-establish contact he has resisted this.

Please know that I am not someone to be ashamed of. I've led a full and often happy life, experiencing a lot of really amazing things. I have a lot to give. If you remember me from the funeral you'll know that I'm a normal unremarkable woman. Your father thinks he is protecting you from me, but we live in a very different world to the one he perceives. Whatever he thinks is the threat I pose to you, simply doesn't exist. He is haunted by his own fears and insecurities.

Please don't be angry with your father. His fight is with me, not with you. I hope one day he will mellow and let me back into his life, and maybe you can help with that. I've tried many times to get him to accept me, but have had so many failures I've almost given up trying. My last conversion ended in a blazing row, when I tried to suggest family counselling. As always, I was being calm and measured and trying to come up with suggestions on how to move forward. I thought this was an excellent suggestion, but I think he saw it as me putting the blame on him, by suggesting he needs therapy, and he became very angry. He has issues. The solution lies with him. I can't not be who I am: I can't become his brother. In fact, in a very real sense, I was never his brother, I was always his sister. I think deep down he sees that.

I think he has concerns about what his pupils will do if they find out his sister is trans. I think he worries what your school friends will do when they find out about your *tranny* aunt. Firstly, is anybody really bothered these days? Secondly, why would anybody ever find out? I have lots of friends and colleagues who have no idea I'm trans. Why would a load of kids who don't even know I exist find this out?

Your father met me recently. It was only the third time we had met face to face since my transition. For the first time we had a chance to sit down and discuss things privately. He said that with me *as I am now* he could see us having a future. I have been *as I am now* for 28 years, so I think what he meant was that because I wasn't how he feared I might be - some pathetic figure of ridicule - then he was prepared to give things a go. What worried me though, was that he had just handed me your grandma's jewellery, which I'd always been promised, and had given me a copy of your grandad's will, to prove I had been left nothing by him, and so he had rid himself of all obligations to me. As he left he said "I'll have to decide if I ever want to see you again". That didn't sound like a man who was prepared to move forward.

The day after that meeting was our row about family counselling. He became very angry and defensive. That was the last I heard from him.

I know your mother is trying to help your father come to terms with what's happened between us. I think your mother needs help from the two of you; there doesn't seem much I can do to assist.

I have a great capacity for love. I could be a benefit to any family. Because of who I am, I've never really felt part of any family. As a child I felt detached and unloved; knowing I was trans, I felt ashamed and unlovable. My parents were responsible for some of these feelings, by the way they reacted whenever they saw behaviour in me that didn't meet with the required gender norm for a boy. It was incredibly difficult as a girl to fit in with the expectations of being a boy, and that drove a wedge between us. Your grandad became openly hostile towards me when he found out I was trans. Relationships broke down to the extent that he vowed never to mention me ever again, and he never did. What family I had ceased to exist from that moment forth.

Your father was a victim of sorts. I transitioned while he was at university. I didn't have a phone number for him, and no address. My only contact was by writing via our parents, but they threw my letters away. They were in contact with the doctors at Charing Cross Hospital who were treating me. I had hoped that the doctors would help the family understand that this wasn't some whim of mine, but was a recognised condition: it was just the way I am, just as my eyes are slate green, and my top wisdom teeth have never appeared. The way the doctors reacted though, and I've only just found this out from your father and it makes me angry, was to tell the family to let me go and leave me alone to transition on my own. That certainly explains a lot, but tell that to someone like your father and his father, and they use it to justify their actions in not wanting to deal with the situation. Now they can just cast me out and not feel guilty - the doctors told them to.

You are both intelligent boys and capable of dealing with this. I wouldn't want to burden you with trying to bring us back together, but just your simple understanding and acceptance of me would go a long way to repairing the damage.

Harry, I've watched your gymnastics on YouTube - truly breathtaking. You are incredibly gifted. I wish you all the best in your international aspirations. Remember it takes dedication: if you truly want to succeed then you must commit yourself fully to it. If you really want it, then you can do it. I too was an international competitor: I represented Great Britain at windsurfing. I lived and breathed the sport for five years and rose to fourteenth in the world. Looking back I used to have regrets at not achieving more. Balancing what I achieved though against having a full time job, I did remarkably well. I now have no regrets. If you can look back in years to come and say you have no regrets, then you have lived a good life.

Robert, you are a talented musician. I wish you all the best in whatever you choose to do with those skills. I won't pretend to have anything like your talent, but I have published CDs of my music and had glowing praise on Dublin's XFM chillout show. Like my comments to Harry, if you truly want to succeed then devoting yourself to your passion for music will get you there. Maybe one day I can introduce you to my collection of classic vintage synthesisers.

You're two great kids. I hope I will be able to share in your amazing lives. Please know that I am here whenever you want to contact me. You two are the closest I have to children of my own, and there will always be a place in my heart for you.

Your loving aunt,

Anne

# You're not trans anymore

I've recently been emerging from the shadows of twenty seven years of stealth living and into the light of advocacy for the rights of trans people. I feel a calling to help others perhaps not so fortunate as myself. This has involved outing myself to some small degree, but largely within the LGBT community. I anticipate outing myself more and more, but I'm as yet undecided on the extent of my exposure. I feel passionate about fighting the inequalities faced by trans people and helping to end transphobia in whatever way I can. Consequently I have been talking about some of the issues with my family: something I've never really done before.

This has had some unexpected consequences.

Apart from my parents and brother, my family have always been very supportive of me. The only time I've ever had any issues was when my cousin appeared reluctant to take my old name off the rather extensive family tree he had compiled, despite me sending him my re-issued birth certificate.

As I was explaining to them some of the things I'd been involved with, I could see that they were uneasy. It seemed like they were being exposed to a world they knew nothing about. Suddenly they said something which really took me aback:

"But why are you doing this? You're not trans anymore."

I was shocked. To them I was cured and there was no need to dwell on the past. Suddenly my faith in their support of me was badly shaken. It seemed they were ok with me as a woman, a cis woman if you will, but couldn't accept me as a trans woman.

I guess I've not really "been trans" for some twenty seven years, living a life of total stealth and so, in effect, the life of a cis female. If I choose to say I'm not trans then that is my decision and mine alone. When someone else tells me I'm not trans then that rings alarm bells in me. It would be nice to not be trans but society doesn't work like that: every visit to the doctor, every new relationship I enter into to, I'm reminded that I can't leave my history behind. I don't want to leave my history behind though. I want people to see me as I am: an everyday woman with trans history.

Why is being trans so hard to accept? It seems we are tolerated so long as we are ignored. I'd suffered my own version of trans erasure.

Trans erasure is an expression often used in trans activism circles: the act of ignoring the needs or existence of trans people. Stonewall UK do it when they take money raised for LGBT causes and only represent LGB people. The American government and Human Rights Campaign did it when originally drafting the Employment Non Discrimination Act: the inclusion of trans rights was considered too much of a hard sell so trans rights were left out. The press do it when Equal Marriage becomes Gay Marriage, and the terrible injustice under the old law forcing married couples to divorce, if a transitioning spouse is to have their gender legally recognised, fails to be reported on[27]. My own company, a leading IT firm, listed high in the Stonewall top ten ( see previous points ), do it when their LGBT information pages are LGB...LGB....LGB..LGB.....LGB...(I'm working on changing this).

Trans erasure comes in more subtle forms too, when writers use words like *those with ovaries* or *vagina-owners* instead of *women* ignoring trans women and likely upsetting some cis women too. It is trans erasure when the existence of trans men is ignored, often because it doesn't suit a particular narrative justifying transphobic hate towards trans people.

It wasn't until I'd had the "you're not trans" conversation with the rest of my family that I fully understood what my brother had said to me after my father's funeral.

---

[27] Now that the Marriage (Same Sex Couples) Act has gone through we have the terrible injustice that a spouse has a veto on the Gender Recognition Certificate of the transitioning partner so they don't get forced into a same sex marriage, which clearly the government doesn't see as equal to an opposite sex marriage. Trans people yet again get short changed.

"We can't move forward if you keep talking about the past."
My family would rather ignore the fact that I'm trans and just treat me as the woman I am; that's great, but it ignores a whole side of my experience. As you'll gather from reading this book, being trans is present in everything I do; as much as I'd like to forget my past, I can't. My past has shaped the person I am; I'm trans and am happy with that; I like myself and am proud of the journey I've taken to get here. Acceptance of oneself is far more important than the acceptance of others.

If I choose to come out more widely, how will my family react? My reading of the situation is that they are happy to accept me while the rest of the world are unaware of my trans history, but would be rather less accepting if everyone knew they had a trans woman in the family. Just as with my parents, my family seem concerned about what other people might think.

This all comes down to society's perception of trans people. If society were fully accepting of trans people then my family would have nothing to be ashamed of.

I have tried to estimate how many people know me: I came up with a figure of two thousand but this figure may be on the low side. I have all the people who knew me from windsurfing, including the spectators at the various championships such as the prestigious World Cup event in Brighton. Over the years I've worked on a lot of different projects with my IT company, bringing me into contact with many colleagues and clients. I coach at a large athletics club and run in most of the local races. As I write this I now think two thousand may be a huge underestimate. The point is that most of these people think they don't know a trans person, as I'm not out to any of them, and they probably don't know anyone else.

The image most folk have of trans people is what's been fed to them from the media. The press appear to have an agenda, representing trans people in a very negative way. They are only interested in sensational stories, stories of regret, stories of how we must protect the children from these deviant people. They seem to regard trans people as the one minority who are still a legitimate target; they regard it as freedom of speech to print articles promoting hatred of trans people.

The entertainment industry are no better: we are portrayed as criminals, serial killers, prostitutes, porn stars, freaks, weirdos and the comedy element, there to spice up the storyline.

It is impossible to be "not trans anymore" when I'm constantly hit by images in the papers and on television that are hurtful and harmful to my sense of self-worth. While I've become hardened to media abuse, others aren't so thick-skinned, and these images can be very harmful to vulnerable trans people, particularly before and during transition. Meanwhile a subliminal image of us is built up in the rest of the population that we are somehow harmful to society and should be kept in our place.

Attitudes towards us are better than they were when I transitioned in 1985 but we still have a long way to go. We must call out bad journalism and injustice wherever we see it; the more of us shout, the more we will be heard. Trans voices used to be a tiny murmur that no one could hear, but we are getting louder by the day and people are starting to listen. I've added my voice to the quiet roar.

Hopefully one day I'll be able to sit back and realise that "I'm not trans anymore". That day is a long way off, but I hope that I will get to see it.

# The Maui turtle

I have a coping mechanism. When times are tough I take myself away to my own little fantasy island and walk on golden sands in the sunlight.

When I was a little girl, I was Ursula Andress, or perhaps I should say Honey Ryder[28], with her conch shell, walking up a Caribbean beach. I wasn't *underneath the mango tree* with *me honey and me* though, as I was always alone: no Sean Connery for me. There was no one to hurt me or tell me who I should be. I was free to be the woman I always knew I was.

For the last fifteen years, my fantasy island has been real.

After retiring from windsurfing competition I continued windsurfing purely for fun, enjoying riding and jumping my local waves. I'd had a generous bonus at work, and with the money burning a hole in my pocket I happened across a luxury windsurfing holiday on the Hawaiian island of Maui. The island's north shore is legendary amongst windsurfers for venues such as Ho'okipa Beach Park, with its big clean waves, and the surf break Jaws, with its monster winter waves featured in the opening sequence of the Bond film *Die Another Day*. (I wonder if all my tropical fantasies revolve around Bond films?)

A few months later I found myself in a million dollar apartment right on the beach at Sprecklesville, perhaps the most perfect all-round windsurfing beach in the world. The modern apartment had a beautifully manicured lush green lawn. Where the lawn ended, the golden sand beach started. The beach framed a small bay ringed by palm trees, with an ancient driftwood half-tree positioned poetically in the middle of the beach, evoking images of Robinson Crusoe desert islands. The warm waters on the inside were calm turquoise, protected by the reef ringing the outside of the bay. The

---

[28] Ursula Andress was walking up that beach, filming Dr No, just one month after I was born.

trade winds played across the bay at the same angle as the prevailing winds on the UK south coast, making me feel very at home in the waves. One could choose to play in the flat water on the inside, ride the waves on the outside, or go blasting across flat water to hit the waves at full speed and so get some huge jumps. This truly was paradise.

For much of the week the waves on the reef to the right of the bay had been the best, and we would sail upwind to make the most of them. Then one day the angle of the surf changed and the waves seemed better to the left: this made for perfect conditions as the geometry of the bay matched the angle of wind and waves perfectly. During my first ride of the day I was at full speed, maybe thirty knots, when suddenly a perfect jumping ramp of a wave popped up in front of me; I kicked off the wave and all my momentum was converted skyward. That was the highest jump of my life and I confess I didn't have the guts to stay with my board and land it: I let go of board and sail and plummeted from great height into the crystal clear waters. I had quite a swim to get back to my board but it was worth it: what a buzz!

I headed out to the reef on the left side of the bay to catch some waves. I had to be careful about the line I chose, as the reef was sucking dry as the waves passed. There was a real danger I could break the fin out of the board if I went too far left; falling onto a coral reef was not something I wanted to contemplate as they are very sharp and would cut me to ribbons.

I popped my board up and over the first wave, on a line I judged to be clear of the reef. As I crested the wave and the foam dispersed, a rock popped up directly in front of me. To my astonishment the rock popped its head out of the water and looked directly at me.

It was as if time stood still. The turtle's eyes were fixed on mine. I'm guessing a turtle's beak gives all turtles a rather surprised expression, but my turtle certainly did look rather shocked to see me hurtling towards her (or him). It was an incredible moment of bonding. I'd never seen a turtle before, and to have one staring straight at me such a short distance away was really rather magical. It was like we connected; I'd never experienced something like that before. It seemed like I was able to dwell on that moment and freeze the experience. It had quite a profound effect on me.

Back to reality and I needed some quick avoiding action: I pulled up on my toes and carved the board upwind away from my beautiful turtle. She popped her head down and was gone.

My holiday on Maui was magical, with so many memories of incredible sailing, rain forests, waterfalls and volcanoes, but my most cherished memory is of my turtle. Whenever I'm feeling down, I can just think back to that one fleeting moment on a reef in paradise and I instantly smile.

My life has had its highs and lows: just being allowed to be me has been an incredible high. The lows have never seemed too deep, but there has been darkness. I've always been able to come back to my happy place, no matter what life has thrown at me. I'll always have my little bit of sunlight in the darkness.

# Conclusion: coming out, part 4

In the chapter *The Fear* I mused over the outcome of outing myself to the man I'd been dating for six weeks. On 14th December 2012 I tested whether those fears were founded.

We met on an online dating site. I'm guessing most dating sites work in a similar fashion, having a set of questions that establish a person's profile, interests, and personality, and provide some measure of compatibility. I chose this particular site because one of the questions is "Would you date a transsexual?". I'd scanned a lot of profiles and all the respondents had answered ***no***. Given the image presented of us in the media, I'm not surprised that most men say they wouldn't date a trans woman. I decided that a reasonable guy would see past the media brainwashing and see me for who I am: one rather hot woman!

I'll qualify that last statement by saying that I've never felt terribly confident about my looks and desirability; being well into my second decade of single celibacy hasn't helped. I was determined though to get back on the dating horse, and hopefully gain sufficient confidence to hang on and not get thrown off. So here I was dating Dave, and trying to time my moment of disclosure.

After discussions with a friend, we'd decided that the moment to tell him was after my Christmas party. I'd invited him to my running club's Christmas bash, where there would be fifty of my friends, and no one would know I'm trans. It seemed that having him witness me in my usual social sphere, in full stealth mode, would help to emphasise that I'm just a regular girl leading a normal life.

After the party we went home and I sat him down on the sofa.
"Dave, there's something I have to tell you: I'm trans. I had a vaginoplasty in my early twenties."
There was a pause while he took that in, but amazingly he didn't react so I added: "You do understand what I mean by that?"

"Yes I do, but you're a woman, you've had some work done, and that's fine."
He then kissed me. He kissed me in all sorts of places!

I'd had a speech ready about respecting him, and wanting to move our relationship on, based on openness and trust, but I did not need to bother. All I needed to add after his initially well behaved advances was "You are allowed to explore a bit you know!".

When we eventually came up for air, I got to hear his side of the story: he'd been concerned that he wasn't good enough for me, being older and a bit overweight. This was a revelation to me: I'd never dreamed that it would be the other person in the relationship who had the issues! I felt so sorry for him as he told me his insecurities. He thinks he's really lucky to have found me.

Whenever I've come out to someone I can't help but look for the little signs that show that they are accepting of me, or otherwise. Dave is given to public displays of affection, something I've never experienced before; while I might not yet be completely comfortable kissing in public, it shows me that he is very accepting of me.

So, dear reader, did you want a happy ending? It looks like there are reasonable people in this world who find me attractive and dateable, people who do not recoil in horror at the thought of someone crossing the gender divide. I can't promise you happy ever after, but the view looks pretty good from here.

My life continues beyond the scope of this book, and is entering exciting times. I am emerging from the shadows and telling my story. I've come out to many people during the writing of the book and they have all been positive experiences.

One day I'd like the whole world to see that trans people are just ordinary people.

But please, never accuse me of being ordinary!